Steps to Better Writing

aspects
of
english

Steps to Better Writing

a systematic approach to
expository writing

Gene Stanford

HOLT, RINEHART AND WINSTON, INC.

NEW YORK • TORONTO • LONDON • SYDNEY

The Author

GENE STANFORD holds an A.B. in English from Washington University and an M.A. in Counseling from the University of Colorado, where he is currently an NDEA Doctoral Fellow in the School of Education. He is the author of *Stanford/McGraw-Hill Vocabulary* and is coauthor of *Learning Discussion Skills Through Games*, *Human Interaction in Education*, and *Myths and Modern Man*. He has compiled several literature anthologies, including *Generation Rap* and the *New World Issues* series.

Copyright © 1972 by Holt, Rinehart and Winston, Inc.
All Rights Reserved
Printed in the United States of America
ISBN 0-03-076490-4
 789   008   10

To the Teacher

As any English teacher knows, most composition texts aren't really very helpful in teaching the average student how to write. They neither present the basic principles of composition in a manner he can readily comprehend, nor allow him to build his knowledge step-by-step—grounding new principles in what he has already learned. These texts assume that the student already knows intuitively how to apply such complex concepts as "unity" and "development" or how to differentiate between "specific" and "general" in a writing situation. While they often flood him with pages of detailed discussions on *how* to write, they rarely require the student to do much practice on his own. Moreover, most composition books demonstrate the principles of composition with polished "literary models" from magazines and books—examples which may represent the acme of expository writing, but which many students can't even follow, let alone appreciate and emulate. Such texts—years behind their equivalents in math and science—apparently assume that the student will simply absorb these explanations and examples and then magically apply them when he finally sits down to write his own paragraph or essay.

Such failings in most texts are significant, but the good teacher can overcome them in one way or another. However, there is one shortcoming that is more difficult to handle: the requirement that the teacher introduce, explain, and supervise nearly every step of the learning process. In this day of flexible scheduling, increased emphasis on independent study, and other innovative teaching practices—to say nothing of the staggering work load composition teachers have always had to carry—a self-teaching self-checking text is desperately needed.

This workbook attempts to fill that need. Thirty-three exercises break down the skills of composition into small steps. Each step includes all the instructions the student needs to do his own work, as well as an answer key that allows him to check his answers. Hence, the student can move at his own rate, practicing each skill, checking his achievement, and determining for himself if he is ready to proceed. In order to give the student opportunities to create wholly original compositions—and to double-check his progress from time to time—some exercises call for complete paragraphs and essays, to be graded by the teacher (*steps 21C, 23, 27, 31*, and *33*, for example). But, in general, left alone with the workbook, the student teaches himself, and the exercises should not be graded.

Because *Steps to Better Writing* is a *work*book, the student spends his energies learning the skills of composition by *writing*, rather than by theorizing or reading models he could never hope to duplicate. It has therefore seemed sensible to base all examples and exercises on typical student writing. No literary models are included. Only a few students can become literary artists; but all high school students can learn to express themselves coherently and effectively if they are made aware of every step of the writing process and given a basic writing formula which they can apply to a multitude of writing situations. To provide these needed tools is the intention of this book.

The author wishes to express his thanks to Marie N. Smith, good friend and colleague, for her encouragement and helpful suggestions during the preparation of the original manuscript. Grateful acknowledgement is also made to the following students for the use of their writing as examples and exercises: Keiley Caster, Richard Weston, Mark Rosenberg, Michael McDowell, Debbie McBride, Jack Whittier, Diane Jaworski, Charles Preston Seiss III, Randy Moresi, Barbara Shapiro, Ricky Shaikewitz, Jack Engler, Bruce Fonarow, Steve Block, Susan Chen, Robert Soell, John Stokes, Howard Mirowitz, Helane Wilen, Jeff Osman, June Westerhold, Mark Pasek, Janet Nebel, Wes Burgess, Sharon Pearline, Edward Thoenes, John Richardson, Marsha Sherman, Ellen Cohen, Lori Glassman, Lindy Gredizer, Mara Goldfarb, Linda Rich, and Booker Green.

Contents

Steps to
Better Writing

step 1. Understanding the Why and How

Few students fail to shudder when a teacher in English or social studies or science assigns an essay or term paper. But the truth is that there is really no need for panic. Essay writing is a simple process, requiring an understanding of only a few basic principles which can be applied in almost every writing situation. It's really not necessary to write by the "plunge" method—holding your nose, closing your eyes, and hoping that the stream of words you produce will be given a decent grade by the teacher. It's possible to learn a step-by-step approach to writing paragraphs and essays, and by following this system to turn out good compositions consistently. This book certainly doesn't claim that any teenager can blossom into a Shakespeare or a Hemingway overnight—if ever. But it does guarantee that you can learn to write a clear, well-organized composition anytime you're required to, without the usual nail-biting anxiety.

step 2. Understanding "Specific" and "General"

Since the terms "specific" and "general" are used throughout this book, it is important to nail down at the beginning exactly what they mean. A *general* word or statement refers to a whole thing or a class or group of things. A *specific* word or statement refers to a part of a whole or one member of a class or group. For example, *boy* is general, while *Jim* is specific. And *I don't like to write essays* is general, while *I can never think of a good topic* is specific. In both of these examples the second item is one particular part of a larger item or class.

Label each of the words, phrases, or statements in each pair below
S *for specific or* G *for general.*

1. ... novel

   ... *Gone with the Wind*

2. ... convertible

   ... automobile

3. ... Los Angeles

   ... city

4. ... clothing

   ... shirt

5. ... school subjects

   ... English

6. ... learning to hold the racket

   ... learning to play tennis

7. ... doing homework

   ... reading the assignment

8. ... my messy room

   ... clothes all over the floor

9. ... attempting to be courteous

   ... holding the door open for girls

10. ... carefully measuring one cup of sugar

    ... making cookies on a Saturday afternoon

11. ... Mr. Robertson is a good citizen.

    ... Mr. Robertson votes in every election.

12. ... There's nothing more exciting than spending the day at an amusement park.

    ... Some people are afraid to ride the ferris wheel.

13. ... Drag racing can be dangerous.

    ... Many people have been killed in drag races.

14. ... Punishment is sometimes used to make a rebellious child obey his parents.

    ... My father uses a belt to whip me when I disobey.

15. ... My favorite vacation is the spring holidays when my family takes a trip.

    ... Students at our school get three weeks of holidays during the year.

16. ... Bob Dixon is our team's best basketball player.

    ... Bob Dixon scored all thirty-six of our team's points in last night's game.

Check your answers on p. 103 before continuing.

step 3. Relating "Specific" and "General"

A word or statement is never always specific or always general; it depends on what other word or statement it is compared to. For example "tree" is *general* when compared to "oak," since "tree" is the group or class to which "oak" belongs. But "tree" is *specific* when compared to "plant," since "tree" is only one member among many in the class "plant."

Number the items in each list below in order of increasing specificity. Place a 1 beside the most general term, a 2 beside the term which is somewhat more specific, a **3** *beside the term which is even more specific, and so on.*

1. ... planet

   ... house

   ... street

   ... state

   ... nation

   ... city

2. ... Tim

   ... male

   ... animal

   ... human being

   ... boy

3. ... studying grammar

   ... going to school

   ... attending my boring classes

   ... spending hours in English class

   ... making subjects and verbs agree

4. ... trying on countless stylish dresses

   ... purchasing an attractive new blue dress

   ... going shopping

   ... looking through the department stores downtown

   ... finally arriving at the last store—Miller's

5. ... I have a lot of fun on weekends.

... At a recent party we learned a new dance step, the "funky chicken."

... Of all the ways to spend a Saturday night, I like parties best.

... Dancing at parties is fun.

... A teenager enjoys his leisure time.

6. ... Both the school and the students suffer from too much involvement in extracurricular activities.

... My friend Tom was hurt academically by his participation in so many sports activities.

... Extracurricular activities can prevent a student from doing well in his classwork.

... Tom failed three courses during football season because he neglected his homework in favor of football practice.

... Extracurricular activities can be harmful to the student.

7. ... I prefer traveling by automobile to any other form of travel.

... My family has always owned Chevrolet cars, which are very comfortable on long trips.

... I feel that American cars are designed better for travel than foreign cars.

... My favorite pastime is traveling.

... We now have a bright red Chevrolet convertible—great for summer vacations!

8. ... Slaves were generally sold at auctions, in the same manner as cattle or hogs.

... Most historians believe that there were many reasons for the Civil War.

... Often a good slave would sell for as much as $1500.

... One reason for the Civil War was the South's refusal to abolish the lucrative practice of black slavery.

... The Civil War was an important historical event in America.

Check your answers on p. 103 before continuing.

step 4. Adding Up Specifics

When a number of specifics are "added together," we can label the group with a general term. For example, if we add together *Bill, Tim, John, Sam, Mike* and *Bob*, we get the general term *boy*. Or if we add together *Ford, Plymouth, Chevrolet, Buick*, and *Volkswagen*, we come up with the general term *automobile*. Another way of arriving at a generalization is to ask yourself, "What do all of these terms have *in common*? Is there perhaps a *special* way in which they are related?" Fords, Plymouths, Chevrolets, Buicks, and Volkswagens have in common the fact that they are all automobiles, and so the general term is *automobile*. (A group of specifics may be related in more than one way, such as in the case of the first example above, where the general term *first name* may be substituted for *boy*.)

EXERCISE A. *Circle the letter of the item in each group below that is general enough to include or summarize all the other items.*

1. a) sofa
    b) chair
    c) bed
    d) table
    e) stool
    f) furniture

2. a) oak
    b) elm
    c) pine
    d) tree

e) hickory

f) maple

3.
   a) diagramming sentences
   b) studying English
   c) making book reports
   d) reading short stories
   e) writing paragraphs
   f) learning grammar rules

4.
   a) taking a shower
   b) shining your shoes
   c) getting ready for an important date
   d) combing your hair
   e) making sure your best suit is pressed
   f) shaving

5.
   a) It is easier to park.
   b) It usually requires less gas.
   c) Repair bills are generally lower.
   d) A small car has many advantages over a large one.
   e) License tags are less expensive.

6.
   a) Other guests were the governor of Idaho and the governor of Washington.
   b) Even Lady Baden-Powell, the wife of the founder of Scouting, attended.
   c) Throughout the entire Jamboree the scouts were visited by famous celebrities.
   d) Even the President of the United States was there and spoke on nine different occasions.
   e) Lieutenant Commander Scott Carpenter gave a demonstration on flying at one campfire, and during the rest of Jamboree he worked at the archery range.

7.
   a) I am interested in speed, so the 396 cubic-inch power plant is of special interest to me.
   b) I also like the interior padded dash, thick carpet, and foam-padded bucket seats.
   c) The exterior styling is stunning.

d) The car I would like to own is a hot 1972 Camaro Super Sport.

e) While the Camaro is expensive looking, the price is reasonable enough for the average person to afford.

8. a) The shorter periods resulting from a shortened day would make boring classes easier to tolerate.

b) Everyone would get more sleep.

c) Teachers would have additional time for grading papers and preparing the next day's lesson.

d) Students would have more free time for homework and independent study projects, as well as for out-of-school activities.

e) A shorter school day would benefit both students and teachers.

9. a) The British Hovercraft Corporation has planned a transoceanic vessel that would carry 140 passengers; a freighter hovercraft is also forseeable.

b) Hovercraft—vehicles that ride on a cushion of air produced by downward pointed fans and are driven by propellers—have many intriguing possibilities for the future of transportation.

c) Hovertrains would apply the hovercraft principle to overland travel, operating on concrete thoroughfares at speeds up to 250 miles per hour.

d) Because hovercraft are immune to sonar and torpedoes, they are particularly attractive to the military—especially the Navy and Coast Guard.

e) The perfect vessel for a ferry seems to be a hovercraft because its wide low construction offers plenty of space for automobiles.

10. a) Television broadcasters even control some of the rules under which athletic events are played.

b) The starting time of a game is often delayed or changed to another date to suit the convenience of the television networks.

c) Telecast games must also be stopped frequently for commercials.

d) Television is exercising too much control over athletic events.

11. a) A stream of grapejuice is oozing from the crack in the refrigerator door.
   b) One third of tonight's dinner has been dragged from the counter to the floor.
   c) Unlaced, lying on the table, is an unmated left shoe.
   d) A heap of nursery rhyme books is flung over a pile of newspapers.
   e) Mother is standing exasperated in the doorway.
   f) My two-year-old brother and his security blanket have just plundered the kitchen.

12. a) The school secretary, Mrs. Damron, helps both students and faculty in innumerable ways by writing excuse slips, making announcements, keeping financial records, and assisting in various other tasks.
   b) In the cafeteria, Mrs. Wilson and her assistants plan, prepare, and serve well-balanced meals to over five hundred students daily.
   c) The transportation staff—the bus drivers—is especially important since our school is attended by many students living in far corners of the county.
   d) Also indispensable are the custodians, Mr. and Mrs. Baker, who keep the rooms and corridors clean, repair equipment, and maintain the building.
   e) Behind the scenes at Madison High are many people performing many important jobs.

13. a) A pair of high-topped boots provides needed ankle support.
   b) Proper equipment is important to a good target shooter.
   c) A sling supports the gun and relaxes the tension on arm muscles, thus preventing fatigue.
   d) The shooter's glove is generally made of very soft leather and resembles a knight's gauntlet with the ends of the fingers cut off.
   e) A special jacket with a leather pad near the shoulder helps to keep the butt of the gun from slipping.
   f) Perhaps the most important piece of equipment is a custom fitted gun.

Check your answers on p. 103 before continuing.

EXERCISE B. *In the space provided under each list of specifics below, write a general term (word, phrase, or sentence) which summarizes the list. It may be helpful for you to visualize each list as an addition problem to which you are to supply the answer by "adding up" the specifics. In some instances more than one answer is possible, but choose only one.*

1. boat
    train
    plane
    car
    bus

    GS ....

2. dogs
    cats
    rabbits
    goldfish
    parakeets

    GS ....

3. French
    English
    Spanish
    Japanese
    Italian

    GS ....

4. washing the dishes after dinner
    sweeping off the sidewalk
    making my bed
    helping Dad mow the lawn
    scrubbing the back porch

    GS ....

5. finding a quiet place, away from distractions
    making sure that I have enough light

gathering all the books, materials, and equipment that I need
checking that there is plenty of fresh air

GS . . . .

6. raking leaves in autumn or shoveling snow in winter
babysitting while mother runs errands or goes out at night
working after school in a supermarket or drugstore
washing cars, selling greeting cards, or mowing lawns

GS . . . .

7. Typing is one of the fastest, neatest, and certainly the most
efficient methods of writing available to the student.
Typing consumes less space on the paper than script, enabling
the writer to include more ideas on a page.
This mode of writing presents an ideal opportunity for the
student to improve his grades, since all teachers like easy-
to-read typewritten work.
Since typing is one of the standard requirements for clerical
work, this skill qualifies one for a good summer job.

GS . . . .

8. My driver's education teacher is biting his nails.
With breath held, he covers his face with his hands.
He retightens his seat belt.
His foot hovers unsteadily over the safety brake.

GS . . . .

Check your answers on p. 103 before continuing.

step 5. Perceiving Relationships

*For each pair of charts below, a list of items has been provided. In
the spaces on the charts write the numbers of the items which
would properly fit there. Note that one item has already been*

placed in each chart to give you a hint. This exercise should be a reminder to you that a word (the one given) can be both specific or general, depending on what other word it is compared to.

1. a) transportation
   b) Plymouth
   c) train
   d) plane
   e) Ford
   f) Chevrolet
   g) Dodge
   h) bus

SP. . . . .   SP. . . . .

SP. . . . .   SP. . . . .

SP. . . . .   SP. . . . .

SP. . . . .   SP   car

GS   car   GS . . . .

2. a) daisy
   b) tree
   c) plant
   d) rose
   e) bush
   f) violet
   g) grass
   h) marigold

SP. . . . .   SP. . . . .

SP. . . . .   SP. . . . .

SP. . . . .   SP. . . . .

SP. . . . .   SP   flower

GS   flower   GS . . . .

3. a) visiting the Capitol
   b) sightseeing in New York
   c) spending hours trudging through the Smithsonian Institution

d) traveling through the Midwest
e) touring the United States
f) sightseeing up-hill-and-down in San Francisco
g) walking leisurely under the cherry trees near the Lincoln Memorial
h) touring the White House

SP. . . . .   SP. . . . .

SP. . . . .   SP. . . . .

SP. . . . .   SP. . . . .

SP. . . . .   SP   visiting Washington, D.C.

GS   visiting Washington, D.C.   GS . . . .

4. a) The power loom helped to increase the amount of cloth which could
       be produced each year.
    b) The steam engine provided an efficient, inexpensive means for trans-
       porting goods.
    c) Improvements in agricultural methods made it possible to support
       the large urban populations needed to run factories.
    d) The spinning jenny produced thread faster and more efficiently than
       the hand operated wheel.
    e) Discovery of new uses for natural resources was a contributing
       factor.
    f) Standardized parts helped make mass production possible.
    g) The water wheel introduced a new source of power.
    h) The Industrial Revolution was the result of many events and
       developments.

SP. . . . .   SP. . . . .

SP. . . . .   SP. . . . .

SP. . . . .   SP. . . . .

SP. . . . .   SP   The invention of many
                                                     important machines help-
GS   The invention of many   ed to produce the Indus-
      important machines help-   trial Revolution
      ed to produce the Indus-
      trial Revolution   GS . . . .

Check your answers on p. 104 before continuing.

step **6.** # Supplying Specifics

Supply specific words, phrases, or sentences that could logically be
summarized by the general word, phrase, or sentence provided in
each of the charts below. In other words, list items that "add up"
to the "total" that is given.

1. SP ....

   SP ....

   SP ....

   SP ....

   GS   toys

2. SP ....

   SP ....

   SP ....

   SP ....

   GS   sports

3. SP ....

   SP ....

   SP ....

   SP ....

   GS   washing the car

4. SP ....

   SP ....

   SP ....

   SP ....

   GS   taking part in school affairs

5. SP ....

   SP ....

   SP ....

   SP ....

   GS   reading the newspaper

6. SP ....

   SP ....

   SP ....

   SP ....

   GS   The automobile influences our lives in many ways.

7. SP ....

   SP ....

   SP ....

   SP ....

   GS   A good teacher has certain characteristics.

Check the Answer Key on p. 104 before continuing.

step 7. Finding the General Statement

In each group below, underline the one sentence that is general enough to summarize or include the others.

1. The student of today has many worries. Grades put terrific pressures on him. Meeting his parents' demands is another

source of concern. Many young people worry about the future. Whether or not people like him causes today's teenager much anxiety.

2. We spent hours trudging through the Smithsonian Institution, but the exhibits were interesting and worth the effort. The weather was warm and we enjoyed walking leisurely under the cherry trees near the Lincoln Memorial. Our trip to Washington, D.C. was the high point of the summer. We took a tour of the White House and even caught sight of the President as he came out the front door. My uncle, who works in the Pentagon, showed us through that huge building. I'll bet we walked twenty miles through the long corridors.

3. An American adolescent derives his moral standards from many sources. Of course his parents and home life have the greatest influence on him, for he tends to pattern his behavior after that of his first examples. But the adolescent soon begins to recognize that some of his friends from different backgrounds hold moral standards at variance with his own, and he is affected by these differences. Soon the young person begins to develop his own moral code, influenced by the standards expressed in newspapers, books, magazines, radio, television, movies, and by adults in the community. Religion may also influence the development of a young person's moral beliefs. However, in many cases organized religion has not met this challenge and has presented the adolescent with guidance which is either too outdated or too hypocritical to have any relevance to his life.

4. Using a mass transit system would cost the passenger less than driving his own car, by saving him the price of gas, automobile maintenance, and parking fees. A well-planned mass transit network offers many advantages to a city and its citizens. Mass transit offers an attractive alternative to the building of more highways in the city—which would perhaps lessen burdensome taxes for highway construction and would take up little space in comparison to the highway "jungle." Also, the need for huge parking facilities would be eliminated from city plans, because most people could simply walk from the mass transit station to their work. In addition, the system

would be a source of income for the city as well as for the company operating it. Finally, if the system were well-organized, travelers could avoid the long drive to and from the airport and other distant facilities.

5. Since the alligator is an amphibious creature, it needs a place to swim. The best place to keep such a pet is in a fenced-in pond or small lake. If a pond is not available, a large metal swimming pool will do, provided that the water does not contain large amounts of chemicals. Whether the alligator is kept in a pond or in a pool, there should always be abundant vegetation surrounding the area. Although the alligator is not a herbivorous animal it needs this heavy vegetation as a source of camouflage and protection from the sun. The alligator is a cold-blooded animal; it cannot regulate its body temperature. Therefore, the temperature of the area surrounding it must be kept well above freezing or the reptile will die. An alligator must have a natural-like environment in order to survive in captivity.

6. In many of its limitations, our school's dress code is unfair to students. The code states clearly that there will be no "blue jeans" worn at school. Yet students are allowed to wear green, black, or even pastel jeans. The only color not allowed is dark blue, even though all colors are manufactured by the same company in the same style. Our dress code also prohibits the wearing of such popular fashions as barefoot sandals. The code does not specifically state that sandals are not to be worn. It does state, however, that sandals must be worn with socks, and since that is just not the accepted fashion, it keeps students from wearing sandals to school at all. Furthermore, the dress code forces students to wear clothes which aren't appropriate for the weather. In the heat of May and June, boys must wear long pants. During these humid spring months the classrooms become intensely hot and sticky. The dress code's restriction against shorts in school serves only to aggravate the problem. Because students tend to become very restless when they are uncomfortably hot, having to wear slacks simply makes it more difficult for boys to concentrate in class.

7. One situation which is worse than death is the occasional time that a friend, teacher, or relative loses his faith and

trust in you. If you accidentally double-cross a friend, do not live up to a teacher's expectations, or do something that your parents feel is morally wrong, the feeling of utter failure is one which can leave you in worse shape than a corpse. A second situation of this sort is one in which you watch your best friend change from someone who cares about everything and everyone into a snob and a social climber. It is totally disheartening to realize that the person you were once able to confide in is now someone you are afraid to talk to for fear of being ridiculed or snubbed. Finally, there is the experience of performing badly, which everyone has been through. Whether it's losing the hockey game for your team by making a stupid pass, giving a terrible speech, or not being able to memorize your recital piece perfectly, the feeling you get of wanting to dig a hole and jump into it is worse than death any day. In short, though I don't know what death is like, since I have never experienced it, I am almost certain that some situations in a teenager's daily life are worse than dying.

Check your answers on p. 104 before continuing.

step 8. Writing a Topic Sentence

In the blank provided write a general statement that summarizes all the specific statements in each paragraph below. Make sure your statement is a complete sentence (hint: don't begin any with "Why" or "How"), and that it's general enough to include all of the other sentences.

1. ....

.... Many people think that hunting is a sport limited to older, retired men who have nothing to do, but this is not true. While many elderly men enjoy hunting because it furnishes needed exercise and gives them something to do with their added leisure time, many younger men receive as much enjoyment, if not more, from hunting. And hunting is not limited to males, but it is also enjoyed tremendously by females of all ages. Many a teenage daughter or young wife accompanies her father or husband on hunting trips and often bags as much game as he does.

2. . . . .

. . . . First of all, you should attempt to involve yourself in the process, rather than simply reading passively. Think about the material as you read, don't just plow through it as though repeating the Pledge to the Flag. A good practice is to skim over section headings in the assigned chapter before a more detailed reading. These headings do more than create a pleasing page appearance; they show you how the author has organized his ideas and help you to follow his major points. Reading chapter summaries is also a good way to preview chapters. The chapter headings and any introduction supplied by your teacher will often tend to raise questions in your mind about the material. Be aware of these and any other questions that occur to you as you read, and look for the answers. In addition, take time periodically as you read to recite to yourself what you've learned. Giving yourself a quick quiz or review exercise will help to fix the ideas firmly in your mind. Finally, when you have finished reading the assignment, review the main points by looking over the chapter headings and skimming for the central ideas of the text.

3. . . . .

. . . . If the amateur photographer can sell his photos to a magazine or newspaper, he will find it is most lucrative. Often a publication will pay as much as $100 for a single photograph. The production of humorous or exciting pictures through the use of trick photography is another rewarding part of this hobby. While such pictures may not always sell readily, the amateur still has the satisfaction of having created something unusual. If he enters his photographs in a contest, he stands a chance of winning a monetary award and the accompanying recognition and prestige. Since photography is used both in the mass media and in the fields of science, law, and medicine, the young person who makes photography his hobby is also helping to prepare himself for any number of interesting careers.

4. . . . .
. . . . If some animals were not killed by hunters, they would continue to multiply at a geometric rate, and nature would not be able to keep the species' numbers down. This surplus could cause millions of dollars worth of damage to farmers' crops and to the ecological balance in general. There would be so great a number of these animals that the likelihood of disease epidemics would increase. The result could be very serious health problems, not only for animals, but also for man. When animals are allowed to multiply unrestricted—especially now that man has eliminated so many natural predators—there is often not enough food to go around and they starve. Hunting these animals, therefore, is often more merciful than letting them meet a slow and painful death by starvation or disease.

Check your answers on p. 105 before continuing.

step 9. Eliminating Unrelated Specifics

Cross out the items in each list below that do not belong. That is, eliminate those that don't fall under the category given by the general term.

1. automobiles
   a) Cadillac
   b) Boeing 707
   c) Plymouth
   d) Ford
   e) Pontiac
   f) Greyhound

2. fish
   a) trout
   b) mackerel
   c) salmon
   d) seal
   e) tuna
   f) seagull

3. efficient study habits
   a) taking complete notes
   b) reading textbook assignments carefully
   c) forgetting important assignments by failing to write them down
   d) organizing study time
   e) choosing quiet surroundings with adequate lighting
   f) leaving all work until the last minute
   g) having necessary books and materials at hand to avoid wasting time looking for them
   h) reviewing class notes periodically

4. advantages of having a hobby
   a) It gives you something to do when alone.
   b) My hobby is basketweaving.
   c) Sometimes it can be financially profitable.
   d) It can help you meet people with common interests.
   e) Many people don't have hobbies but they should.
   f) Knowing that you are an expert at something gives you confidence in yourself.
   g) Many hobbies expose you to new and interesting things.

5. advantages of spring vacation
   a) It gives students a chance to recuperate from school pressures.
   b) It allows kids to go on trips with their families.
   c) Students can catch up on schoolwork they may have neglected.
   d) Schools should increase the length of spring vacation.
   e) Private schools have longer spring vacations than public schools.

6. What a good pop music group should have
   a) It should have its own distinct "sound" and not try to imitate other groups.
   b) My favorite group is the Jefferson Airplane.
   c) A good group will get the audience involved in its music.
   d) One of the best features of many good bands is their ability to write their own music.
   e) A good manager is a definite asset to a band.
   f) Today's pop music groups, if they hit it big, can make tremendous amounts of money.

7. There are many things a careful driver does to reduce the possibility of an accident.
   a) He is careful to dim his headlights whenever another car approaches.
   b) A good driver watches the road ahead very carefully, keeping alert for a situation that could lead to an accident, such as a car pulling onto the highway.
   c) To get a license, the driver must pass both a written and a driving test.
   d) He makes sure that his automobile is in top operating condition.
   e) Speeding is sometimes necessary, as in the case of rushing an injured person to the hospital.
   f) A good driver obeys all traffic laws.
   g) Today's cars have too much horsepower to be safe.
   h) He watches out for the mistakes of other drivers.

Check your answers on p. 105 before continuing.

step 10.   Supplying Specifics

Supply at least four specific statements which help to explain or prove each of the general statements below. Be sure that all specifics are directly related to the general statement in question.

1. GS   The life of a movie actor is both exciting and tiring.

   SP ....

   SP ....

   SP ....

   SP ....

2. GS   I have definite ideas about how I would bring up a teen-ager if I were a parent.

   SP ....

   SP ....

   SP ....

   SP ....

3. GS   Driver's training should be a required part of the high school student's education.

   SP ....

   SP ....

   SP ....

   SP ....

Check the Answer Key on p. 105 before continuing.

step 11. Arranging Items in Paragraph Form

Using one of the lists in step 10, write a paragraph. Use the general statement as the topic sentence *and place it first in your paragraph, making sure to indent about one-half inch from the left-hand margin. Support this sentence with the specific statements*

you listed in step 10, *explaining each one in an additional sen-*
tence or two to clarify your meaning. Write the exercise on a
separate sheet of ruled paper.

Check the Answer Key on p. 105 before continuing.

step 12.

Listing Both General Statement and Supporting Specifics

For three of the topics given below, write a general statement in
your own words (as you did in step 4, *exercise B and in* step 8).
Then list at least four supporting specific statements for each (as
you did in step 10). *Make sure your general statement is a com-*
plete sentence; do not *simply copy the topic as it appears here.*
Check each list of specifics to be sure that all explain or prove the
general statement. If there are some which don't, cross them out
and add any others that occur to you.

    a)   My Favorite Pastime (Game, Hobby, Sport)
    b)   Why Reading Is Necessary
    c)   How to Get a Part-time Job
    d)   My Biggest Disappointment
    e)   Getting Along with Teachers

  1. GS . . . .

      SP . . . .

      SP . . . .

      SP . . . .

      SP . . . .

2. GS . . . .

   SP . . . .

   SP . . . .

   SP . . . .

   SP . . . .

3. GS . . . .

   SP . . . .

   SP . . . .

   SP . . . .

   SP . . . .

Check the Answer Key on p. 105 before continuing.

step 13.   Arranging Items in Paragraph Form

Turn one of your list from step 12 *into a paragraph, using your general statement as the topic sentence and your list of specifics to support it. Explain each specific statement with at least one additional sentence, adding any information that helps to connect them. Write your paragraph on a separate sheet of ruled paper, indent the first line of your paragraph about one-half inch from the left margin, and keep your margins on both sides as straight as possible. Then underline the topic sentence and number the specifics in the order they appear in the paragraph, as shown in the following example.*

<u>I enjoy traveling very much.</u> [1]It is exciting to see new and unusual places. But I couldn't see very much if I stayed close to home all the

time. [2]I also find that traveling helps me with my schoolwork. It often introduces me to ideas, people, and places that I later study in my textbooks. [3]I find that travel makes me a more interesting person. I have more things to talk about when with other people, and they seem more interested in what I have to say. [4]But most important, I guess, is that traveling allows me to get away from the boring routine of everyday living. It lets me operate on a different time schedule than I'm used to and lets me do more of what I enjoy doing.

Check the Answer Key on p. 106 before continuing.

Check the Answer Key on p. 106 before continuing.

step 14.

Providing Connecting Information

A good paragraph is more than just a list of specifics following a general statement. It is a unified whole, with ideas that flow from one to the next. In this way it is different from a grocery list. To help connect your ideas, you should fill in the gaps between them with explanation. You should also let the reader know how the different ideas are related to each other. In *steps 11* and *13*, you were instructed to explain each specific statement with at least one additional sentence. Often it will require more than one extra sentence to explain and connect the specific statements.

EXERCISE A. *Check the paragraphs you wrote for* steps 11 *and* 13 *to see whether you have provided adequate connecting explanation. Do your ideas flow from one to another or are there awkward gaps or interruptions between the specifics? Does your paragraph sound like a grocery list or is it a unified whole? Sometimes it is difficult to detect these things in your own work. Ask a friend to read your paragraph for this purpose and to indicate where you need better connectors. Then rework these spots and ask your friend to check them again.*

EXERCISE B. *In the following paragraph only the main ideas supporting the topic sentence have been included. Fill in the blanks with connecting explanation in order to turn this "grocery list" into a smooth-flowing paragraph. (Topic sentence underlined.)*

<u>While television shows are reasonably good, the commercials that accompany them are a disgrace.</u> [1]One of the many bad features of commercials is their loudness. ....

.... [2]Commercials take up too much time and are repeated too often. ....

.... [3]Often commercials interrupt a show at a particularly inappropriate time. ....

.... [4]Too many commercials insult the viewer's intelligence by presenting unrealistic situations and senseless dialogue. ....

Check the Answer Key on p. 106 before continuing.

step 15.

Writing a Complete Paragraph

Carefully plan and write a paragraph, following the steps below and checking them off as you do them.

...1. Choose one of the following topics.
   a) Courtesy Is Necessary (Hypocritical) in Our Society
   b) The Definition of a Good Sport
   c) The Needless Emphasis on Grades
   d) Male Chauvinism Is (Is Not) a Fact of Life in America
   e) An Unfair Rule

...2. Using the following chart, plan your paragraph. Write a general statement about your topic in the blank provided. Make sure it's a complete sentence and shows your opinion on some aspect of the topic. Then list at least four specifics which support your general statement.

   GS ....

   ....

   SP ....

   SP ....

   SP ....

...3. Check your list of specifics to make sure they are all directly related to your general statement. Do they all help to prove or explain it? If any of your specifics do not belong, cross them out. Add any others you think of.

...4. Write your paragraph on a separate sheet of ruled paper, being sure to explain each specific statement with one or two additional sentences containing whatever material is needed to connect your ideas.

...5. Check your paragraph for any errors in grammar, punctuation, and spelling. Then underline the topic sentence and number the specifics (see *step 13*). Of course you will not always do this last step in writing a paragraph to turn in to your teacher. But, when practicing, it helps you to visualize the structure of your paragraph.

Check the Answer Key on p. 106 before continuing.

step 16.   Positioning the
                             General Statement

In all of the exercises thus far, you've been placing the general statement (the *topic sentence*) of your paragraph at the beginning. This is the usual procedure. But sometimes it is useful to save the general statement until last. In this type of paragraph you begin with specifics and end with the generalization that summarizes or draws a conclusion from them. Here is an example of a paragraph with the topic sentence at the end.

> A self-confident person is one who knows he will succeed; a conceited person isn't so sure, but he tries to make it appear that he is. The conceited person constantly lets everyone know that he's tops, while the truly self-confident person doesn't have to advertise himself. He knows that people will accept him for what he is and not for what he may seem to be, and he simply tries to make as good a person of himself as he can. But the conceited person's behavior is caused by a basic insecurity about being accepted. Therefore, it becomes apparent that the difference between a self-confident person and a conceited one is that the conceited person has no self-confidence. (*Topic sentence underlined.*)

Sometimes it's useful to place the generalization or topic sentence at the beginning of the paragraph in order to let the reader know immediately what the paragraph is about, and then to restate the generalization at the end as a summary and conclusion. This type is sometimes referred to as a *sandwich paragraph*, since the specifics are "sandwiched" in between two statements of a general idea. (The general statement at the end is often called a *clincher* sentence because it ties together the details in the paragraph.) Here is an example of a sandwich paragraph. It begins with a general statement (topic sentence), then presents supporting details, and concludes with a restatement of the general idea (clincher).

> Parents should guide their children in growing up. While the child is still quite young, he should be given a few simple responsibilities, such as keeping himself clean without always having to be told to. Later, parents should help him learn to manage some of his other affairs, such as budgeting his allowance and deciding on a sensible bedtime. By the time he reaches adolescence, parents should have prepared him for the more important decisions he will have to make—whether he wants to go

to college, whether to experiment with drugs, and so forth. <u>Learning</u>
<u>to accept responsibility, to manage ones own affairs, to make one's own</u>
<u>moral and professional decisions are important steps in growing up, and</u>
<u>parents have an obligation to prepare their children to take them.</u> (*Topic*
sentence and clincher underlined.)

EXERCISE A. *In each paragraph below, underline the topic sentence (general statement). It may be at the beginning, or at the end, or in some cases at the beginning with a clincher at the end (if so, underline both).*

1. The owner of a pet alligator should protect it by placing it in a pen of some sort. The most dangerous enemies of such a pet are human beings. Young neighborhood children will attempt to do away with the murky green reptile by squeezing and squishing it, by feeding it inedible items, by stoning it, or simply by scaring it to death. Other animals are also adversaries of a pet alligator. Both cats and dogs will be curious about this strange looking creature. When investigating it to satisfy their curiosity they may challenge the alligator. Still another major threat to its existence in civilization is traffic. Nowadays, with the increase in cars, trucks, and bicycles, the chances for a pet alligator on the lose are not good. All of these dangers can be eliminated if the owner keeps his pet in a fenced off pond or in a pen.

2. The important question of whom to have as a friend must be answered by the teen himself—not by his parents. It's unfair for parents to forbid their child to see Tom, Dick, or Harry on the basis of mere gossip. They must have faith that their teen will have the good judgment to choose friends on the basis of what he knows about them personally, not on rumor. Of course, there is a good chance the teen may discover that his judgment hasn't been good and, if the parent dosen't interfere before this time, he will usually find plenty of ways to avoid an undesirable person. If parents have faith in the teenager's judgment they will generally find that it pays off in the long-run, because the child will often choose friends sensibly and, even when he makes a mistake, he can learn much from it.

3. An understanding of history helps us to realize that our problems are nothing new. Up to and during the Civil War period, for example, there was the problem of discrimination against

the Negro; in the year 1972 he is still fighting for equality. Similarly, there have always been groups of people trying to be nonconformists. During the 1920's and 1940's they were the "flappers" and "zoot-suiter," who were looked upon as quite eccentric. Today people are still rebelling against society and trying to be different, but now we call them "hippies." The problem of young men dying in war has always existed. During the first and second world wars, thousands of soldiers were killed. Today, unfortunately, young men are still dying on the battlefield. The only things that have changed are the locations and the weapons. Clearly, today's problems aren't really so new; they simply appear in different forms.

4. Good notetaking is indispensable to efficient study. When it's time to take notes, don't grab any piece of paper that happens to be handy and begin to scribble. Instead, keep a special section of your notebook for all your notes on each subject. Label each set of notes with the class, and the date, and the name of the lecture so that you'll be able to put it back in its logical order should you have to remove it from the notebook for some reason. For maximum efficiency, make a real effort to discriminate between the important and the trivial in what you hear. Don't just write all you can, as fast as you can. Instead, listen for main points and supporting details. Putting your notes in outline form is also helpful. Avoid the "stream of consciousness" style that so many students use—long paragraphs of unrelated ideas, including cryptographic notations of various comments by the instructor. You will find it helpful to look over your notes as soon as possible after taking them in order to revise or rewrite them intelligently. This step prevents the horrible realization the night before a test that "My notes just don't make sense!"

5. My greatest disappointment, I think, was the time I went to camp in Vermont. When I first got there it was night and I couldn't see too much, but I did see clearly the small cabin with no windows and half a door which let in all the cold air every night. I had to sleep with six blankets. In the morning I walked down to the stables. The picture of the stables in the pamphlet I had received must have been taken twenty or more years ago, and was very misleading—showing the stables bright and shiny, when in reality they were broken

down and in need of paint. After that, I walked up to the so-called lake, which was really a dirty pond with a cement bottom. Again, the picture in the pamphlet had been misleading. The next day I found out that there wasn't as much horseback riding as that pamphlet had implied—and the riding had been my main reason for choosing the camp! Perhaps my experience would have been less disappointing had I known before I arrived what the camp was really like.

6. The Gateway Arch, a national monument to the westward expansion movement, is located in downtown St. Louis on the Mississippi River, and is 630 feet high. The height is amazing; you can see the arch from as far as twenty miles away. The spaciousness of the rooms underneath is also fantastic. There are two movie theaters, a fountain in the middle of a lobby, and a museum—all underground. The train that takes visitors to the top is a pure engineering feat. It turns like a ferris wheel seat as it moves up the horseshoe curve in the arch. The view at the top is wonderful. You can see every building, smokestack, and main street in downtown St. Louis and across the river to East St. Louis. The Gateway Arch is a truly spectacular tourist spot.

7. Often the starting time of a sports event is delayed or changed because of television. Such an instance occurred last fall in a college football game between Syracuse and Penn State. The game was being televised and ABC network control personnel thought it would be best if the game were started forty-five minutes late so that more viewers would be attracted. Unfortunately the stadium did not have any lights and by the end of the game the two teams were groping around in the dark. An equally disturbing event involved Southern Methodist University and Texas A and M. For the last twenty-two years these teams have traditionally clashed on Thanksgiving Day. This year, however, they met on September 16th, just so the game could be televised.

8. Typing is much less fatiguing than handwriting, especially when you use an electric typewriter. You can typewrite for hours without fatigue, while steady writing for a time will often produce writer's cramp. Also, no matter how tired you become, the character of typed letters never changes. Script,

on the other hand, will tend to get sloppy after long periods of writing. Furthermore, typing is always legible with a minimum of effort. At times personal script is so poor that it is difficult, if not impossible, to read. Legibility can contribute to an improved grade, since a teacher is more likely to give a low grade to a sloppily written paper than to a neat, typewritten one. The biggest advantage, however, is speed. A good typist can type from forty to seventy words per minute, while you can write only about twenty to thirty words per minute by hand. Every high school student, therefore, should learn to type because of the many advantages which typing has over script.

Check your answers on p. 106 before continuing.

EXERCISE B.   *Carefully plan and write a paragraph, placing the topic sentence at the* end. *Follow these steps, checking them off as you go:*

... 1.   Choose one of the following topics:
   a)   Kinds of People Who Irritate Me
   b)   What I Want in a Friend
   c)   What It Takes to Be a Good Athlete
   d)   The Worries of Teenagers

... 2.   Using the chart below, plan your paragraph. Write a general statement that expresses your opinion on some aspect of the topic. Make sure it is a complete sentence. Then list at least four specifics which support this general statement.

   GS . . . .

   . . . .

   SP . . . .

   SP . . . .

   SP . . . .

   SP . . . .

... 3.   Check to make sure that all of your specifics are directly related to your general statement. Do they all help to prove or explain it? If any of them do not belong, cross them out. Add any others you can think of.

...4. Write your paragraph on a separate sheet of ruled paper, placing the general statement at the end. (You will therefore begin the paragraph with the first specific, not the topic sentence.) Be sure to explain each specific statement with one or two additional sentences containing whatever material is needed to connect your ideas.

...5. Check your paragraph for any errors in grammar, punctuation, and spelling. Then underline the topic sentence and number the specifics.

Check the Answer Key on p. 107 before continuing.

EXERCISE C. *Plan and write a* sandwich *paragraph, placing the topic sentence at the* beginning *and rephrasing the general statement in a clincher sentence at the* end. *Follow these steps, checking them off as you go.*

...1. Choose one of the following topics.
   a) How to Enjoy a Weekend
   b) The Role of Prison in Society: Retribution or Reform?
   c) The Good (or Bad) Effects of Commercial TV on Children
   d) What Money Can't Buy

...2. Using the chart below, plan your paragraph. Write a general statement about your topic in the space provided. Make sure it's a complete sentence and shows your attitude toward some aspect of the topic. Then list at least four specifics which support your attitude.

GS . . . . , ...

. . . .

SP . . . .

SP . . . .

SP . . . .

SP . . . .

...3. Check your list of specifics to make sure they are all directly related to your general statement. Eliminate any that are not. Add any others that occur to you.

...4. Write the paragraph on a separate sheet of ruled paper, placing the topic sentence at the beginning. Be sure to explain each specific statement with one or two additional sentences containing whatever material is needed to connect your ideas.

. . . 5. Conclude your paragraph with a *clincher* sentence – a restatement of the general idea in different words from the topic sentence and written in such a way as to make your paragraph sound "finished."

. . . 6. Check your paragraph for any errors in grammar, punctuation, and spelling. Then underline the topic sentence and the clincher sentence, and number the specifics.

Check the Answer Key on p. 107 before continuing.

step 17.   Using Four Types of Specifics

Students often can't think of enough specifics to explain their topic sentence, and their paragraphs tend to be a repetition of the general idea without any specific proof or explanation. (The use of specifics to support a topic sentence is sometimes called "development.") A poorly developed paragraph can be avoided if you plan ahead of time to include as many relevant specifics as possible. Often, students think it is difficult to come up with specifics in the planning stage. To avoid this problem you should learn what types of specifics are available. Here are four examples of the most common types.

Examples, Illustrations.   Each of the specifics given below is an example of the "different forms" of soap mentioned in the general statement.

GS   It is possible to buy soap in many different forms.

SP   Cake soap is milled and pressed into a hard, long-lasting cake.
SP   Bar soap is cut from a huge slab of soap by long knives.
SP   Flake soap is scraped from a slab in small, flat pieces.
SP   Powdered soap is formed by condensing crystals on the cold surface of a cooling tower.

Facts, Statistics, Data. Each of the specifics given below is a fact or statistic which helps to prove the general statement.

GS   Although nearly every war has been fought with the idea that it would be the last, the history of civilization has proved otherwise.

SP   From 1500 B.C. to 1860 A.D., there were at least 8000 wars.

SP   Since 650 B.C., there have been 1656 arms races, all but sixteen ending in actual hostilities.

SP   In the 150 years after 1776, Great Britain alone was involved in 54 wars, lasting a total of 102 years.

SP   During that time, France was engaged in 53 wars, lasting for 99 years.

SP   The United States was almost continually in one kind of battle or another: the Revolution, the War of 1812, the Civil War, wars against Indians, the Mexican War, the Spanish-American War, World Wars I and II, and military actions in Mexico, Haiti, Nicaragua, the Dominican Republic, Cuba, and Southeast Asia.

An Incident. Each of the specifics below tells part of a story which explains or justifies the general statement:

GS   I have always been wary of airplane travel, and with good reason.

SP   I remember my first flight on a commercial airline.

SP   It was on a DC-3 from Topeka, Kansas, to Stillwater, Oklahoma.

SP   The stewardess was as nervous as I.

SP   She assured me, however, that the plane could land in a cornfield if necessary—and we almost did!

SP   Despite the rough flying, I manfully ate my dinner—much to my regret.

SP   Our landing gear stuck and we had to circle Stillwater airport using up fuel, before an emergency landing.

Reasons. When the general statement leads the reader to ask "why?", it needs to be explained with reasons, such as those in the example below:

GS   Every high school student should learn to type.

SP   It's faster than writing.

SP   It's neater—helps you get better grades.

SP   It can help you find a summer or part-time job.

SP   It's less tiring than script.

EXERCISE A. *Label each of the specifics listed below as an example, fact, incident, or reason. In deciding, notice the way in which each specific relates to the topic sentence. (Some of the specifics may fall into more than one category.)*

1. Topic Sentence: Our school cafeteria needs improvement badly.

   a) .... SP Only 40 percent of our students choose to eat in the cafeteria.

   b) .... SP One day last week I received a bowl of green beans with a worm in it. When I took the bowl back to the serving line, I was told that I should not be afraid of something as harmless as a tiny worm. I explained that I was not afraid of worms themselves, but considered a bowl of green beans to be an inappropriate place for a worm to take up residence. I was promptly sent to the principal on a charge of "insubordination."

   c) .... SP The average lunch served in our cafeteria costs 25 cents to prepare but is sold for 65 cents.

   d) .... SP The meat loaf is often not cooked long enough.

   e) .... SP The cafeteria is understaffed and poorly managed.

   f) .... SP Students should not be subjected to such an intolerable situation.

2. Topic Sentence: Cigarette smoking is harmful.

   a) .... SP The report on smoking of the Surgeon-General of the United States reveals that smoking increases the likelihood of contracting lung cancer, emphysema, and many other fatal diseases.

   b) .... SP Being a smoker, I am quite familiar with the effects of cigarettes. After having smoked three packs a day for the last 20 years, I find it hard to move about in my hospital bed because I am constantly short of breath; I have a terminal case of lung cancer; and I have bad breath.

   c) .... SP My expenses for cigarettes total almost $400 a year.

   d) .... SP Smoking deprives you of much of the

enjoyment in life. A habitual smoker can't taste a good steak nor can he smell a flower.

e) .... SP   Once, because I had smoked so much, I became so winded after trying unsuccessfully to catch a bus that I didn't have the strength to climb in when the next bus arrived. Consequently, I arrived home four hours late.

3. Topic Sentence: I feel inferior to everyone.

   a) .... SP   My analyst tells me that my inferiority complex is due to unhappy childhood experiences.

   b) .... SP   In eighth grade, a girl once told me that she liked me. I told her that she had to be crazy to like an uncoordinated idiot like me. She promptly walked away with the most profound expression of astonishment on her face that I have ever seen. From that point on, I felt that no one could like me.

   c) .... SP   I am neither intelligent, witty, nor easy to get along with. I'm not especially handsome, I'm no good at sports, and on top of all this I have the worst case of acne ever recorded.

   d) .... SP   People are constantly telling me what a lousy person I am.

Check your answers on p. 108 before continuing.

EXERCISE B. *Underline the topic sentence (and clincher, if there is one,) in each paragraph below. Then decide how each paragraph has been developed (what type of specifics it contains). Only one type has been used in each paragraph. Write your answer in the space provided.*

1. The English language is full of words with Latin roots. The prefix *com-* (meaning "with" or "together") is found in such words as *command, compass, commission, compact,* and *compare.* The knowledge of the Latin word *cedere,* meaning "to yield" or "to go," helps to reveal the meanings of the

English words *cessation, cession, accede, access, ancestor, concede, exceed, incessant, precede, procedure, process, recede,* and *succeed,* as well as many others. Knowing the prefix *uni-* (meaning "one") can help you understand newspaper articles about *unilateral* disarmament, for example. The root *voc-* (meaning "call") will really give you a key to your study of *vocabulary.* In short, a study of Latin roots can expand your knowledge immensely and make you a more literate person.

Type of Specifics ....

2. I feel inferior to everyone. As a child, I was not exactly respected for what I was. My parents were constantly putting me down, and there was nobody to build me back up again. I failed to develop any athletic ability, and was therefore rejected by boys my age. I became shy and withdrawn, putting off people who tried to break through my shell with remarks like "How can you possibly like a worthless person like me?" I never went out on dates because I didn't want to embarrass a girl by forcing her to be seen in public with such a clod. Because of these things, I think of myself as stuck on the bottom rung of the ladder with no way of climbing up.

Type of Specifics ....

3. It has been proven fairly conclusively that the radioactive fallout from nuclear weapons testing shortens the life span of individual organisms. Analysis of death rates in the United States by the Compertz function shows that, for men, the normal life expectancy under normal conditions is cut in half after every increase in age of eight years. Exposure to radiation increases the death rate by shifting the curve of this function to the left. This shift means that the life span will be cut in proportion to the amount of the shift. In particular, a dose of 300 roentgens of radiation shortens the life span by four to nine days per roentgen. Even though the effects are reduced when the dose is spread out over a long period of time, as in the case of fallout, the inescapable conclusion is that radiation definitely affects a population so that its members die off from all causes at earlier ages than they would in a radiation-free environment.

Type of Specifics ....

4. The life of the average citizen in an underdeveloped country is far from pleasant. Only one out of three can read or write. Hundreds of millions live on a dollar a week. The average income is less than $2.50 a week—or $140 a year. (In the United States it is $2800.) Citizens of underdeveloped countries live an average of 36 years; in the United States and Europe the life expectancy is almost twice that—67 years. In 1950, malaria killed a million babies in India alone. Three out of five people in Latin America were discovered never to have had a glass of pure water, and 1000 children a day were dying as a result. Fifty-five out of every 100 children in Guatemala died before the age of four. Thirty million Brazilians did not own a pair of shoes. Hundreds of millions of people in the poorer countries of the world suffered from trachoma, bilharzia, dysentery, anemia, tuberculosis, malaria, leprosy, yaws, and other diseases. Few had a decent roof over their heads. Most lived in mud or bamboo huts.

Type of Specifics . . . .

5. It doesn't take much to prove that women are poor drivers. Once, as I was driving up to an intersection, the car in front of me stopped short. I slammed on my brakes and narrowly avoided a collision. Since the light was green, I honked my horn in an attempt to get the lady to move. As she started to roll slowly forward, the light changed to yellow. She immediately put on her brakes and stopped in the middle of the intersection. I stopped a short distance behind her to enable her to back up. The next thing I knew, the lady's car was moving backwards toward mine at about 60 miles per hour. Before I even had time to honk my horn again, she slammed into my car, giving me a painful whiplash injury.

Type of Specifics . . . .

6. Increasing your vocabulary can help you in a number of ways. You'll discover that knowing synonyms, for example, will decrease the amount of repetition in your compositions and make them more enjoyable to read. And if a teacher enjoys reading your paper, he may even give you a better grade. Also, an increased vocabulary will make your own reading more enjoyable. You'll find it's much easier to follow the ideas in your history textbook or the newspaper when you don't have to continually run to the dictionary to

look up unknown words. If you're not always stumbling over unfamiliar words, you'll become more eager to read and not as discouraged when you *do* come across an unknown word. As a result, you'll read faster and more intelligently, become more knowledgeable, and hence better informed about the world around you. Strange as it may seem, vocabulary study can make you a better person.

Type of Specifics . . . .

7. Often what seems to be a person's weakness can turn out to be a strength. I discovered the truth of this one day last summer. I was sitting on our front porch reading one afternoon when the girl who lives next door came running over. She said that she had locked her baby sister inside her house and that her sister was crying loudly. I went back to her house and saw that the only way to get inside was to climb through the second-floor bathroom window, which was half open. Even if I did manage to climb the tree next to it, I knew I'd never be able to get through the small opening. I began to think like a computer. Suddenly I came up with an idea. I've got a little brother known as Sputnik. Everyone always picks on him because he's small, but he can jump, climb, and run like the devil. I yelled back to our house, "Hey, Sput!" He was there in a jiffy. I told him what he had to do and how to do it. His small size would come in handy when it came time to wiggle through the half-closed window. We watched his every movement as he climbed the tree and leaped to the window ledge. He could barely make it through, but somehow he squirmed in. Once inside, he ran downstairs to the front door and opened it. The girl was so relieved you could see it on her face, Sput was grinning from ear to ear, and I was happy too as I went back to my reading. Sput's being runty had enabled him to do a great thing for the girl next door. His weakness, in this case, turned out to be his strength.

Type of Specifics . . . .

8. One cause of prejudice in our society is the lack of contact between different ethnic, cultural, and economic groups. People who earn about the same amount of money usually live in the same neighborhoods and stick together socially. People with similar cultural and educational backgrounds—

especially immigrants and racial minorities—are very often isolated from the rest of society because they are not accepted by other groups as equals and because they feel happier and safer with those who share the same background and problems. When groups become isolated from each other in this way, fear and distrust builds up. For people who have no social contact with those who are different from themselves can only guess and generalize about the reasons why they act as they do; and more often than not they draw wrong conclusions from ignorance. Nothing is more likely to produce prejudice than trying to judge ideas and behavior one knows nothing about.

Type of Specifics . . . .

9. When parents and children trust and respect each other, the problems that arise between them are much more easily settled than they are in an atmosphere of hostility. I can remember an instance when such mutual respect helped me to maintain a good relationship with my parents. Because they trusted my judgment, my mother and father had given me a set of keys to the car, on the understanding that I would only use it when I had permission. As it happened, I once took the car when I had been asked not to. I could have gotten away with it, but because I realized that this deceit would endanger my relationship with my parents, I told them what I had done. They did not punish me as many parents would have, but respected my honesty and my ability to admit that I had made a mistake.

Type of Specifics . . . .

10. Although most people are aware of the high crime rate in this country and the fact that thousands of people are sentenced to prison each year, few of us have any knowledge of the conditions of prison life. There are about 250,000 men in prisons in the United States. In general, their sentences are longer than any in the Western World. Their lives are harsh and isolated. Many spend long hours doing strenuous manual labor on state farms, yet are given no skills which will enable them to adjust to the outside world. The emotional problems of others make it necessary to keep them in solitary confinement—usually in cells no larger than five feet by nine. As the facilities for rehabilitating prisoners are extremely limited, many return to prison life again and

again. All of these factors seem to point to a self-perpetuating prison system—a sad fact which all too few of us are aware of or concerned about.

Type of Specifics . . . .

Check your answers on p. 108 before continuing.

EXERCISE C. *Plan and write a paragraph developed by* facts *and* statistics. *Follow these steps, checking them off as you go.*

. . . 1. Choose one of the following topics.
   a) The Results of Highway Accidents
   b) Astrology: Science or Superstition?
   c) Oxygen—Essential for the Human Body
   d) The Effects of Tranquilizers (or some other drug)
   e) Our Basketball Team's Fine (or Bad) Season
   f) Marijuana: Is It Really Harmless?

. . . 2. Using the following chart, plan your paragraph. Write a general statement about your topic in the space provided. List the specific *facts* or *statistics* which explain or prove your general statement. (You may have to get your information from a reference book or other outside source.)

GS . . . .

. . . .

Type of Specifics . . . .

SP . . . .

SP . . . .

SP . . . .

SP . . . .

. . . 3. Check to make sure that all your specific details (*facts* or *statistics*) support your general statement directly. Eliminate any that do not.

. . . 4. On a separate sheet of ruled paper, write your paragraph.

. . . 5. Check your paragraph for errors in grammar, spelling, and punctuation. Underline the topic sentence (and clincher if you've used one) and number the specifics.

Check your answers on p. 108 before continuing.

EXERCISE D. *Plan and write a paragraph developed by* examples. *Follow these steps, checking off as you go.*

...1. Choose one of the following topics.
   a) What I Like Most About My Parents
   b) The Tricks of Advertising
   c) How I've Changed Since Junior High
   d) Teachers' Mistakes

...2. Using the following chart, plan your paragraph. Write a general statement about your topic in the space provided. List *examples* which support it.

GS ....

....

Type of Specifics ....

SP ....

SP ....

SP ....

SP ....

...3. Check to make sure that all your specific details are directly related to your general statement. Eliminate any that are not. Add any new ones that occur to you.

...4. On a separate sheet of ruled paper, write your paragraph.

...5. Check your paragraph for errors in grammar, spelling and punctuation. Underline the topic sentence (and clincher if you've used one) and number the specifics.

Check the Answer Key on p. 108 before continuing.

EXERCISE E. *Plan and write a paragraph developed by an* incident. *Follow these steps, checking them off as you go.*

...1. Choose one of the following topics.
   a) Why Students Are Mean to Substitute Teachers
   b) Why Girls Should Share the Cost of Dates
   c) It Doesn't Pay to Take Advice
   d) Worry Is a Useless Activity
   e) My Father's Method of Punishment

...2. Using the following chart, plan your paragraph. Write a general statement about your topic in the space provided. Think of an *incident*—something that proves or explains the general statement. In the appropriate blanks, write the different parts of the incident—the separate events, steps, or various important details that develop your story.

GS . . . .

. . . .

Type of Specifics . . . .

SP . . . .

SP . . . .

SP . . . .

SP . . . .

...3. Check your specifics to make sure you have included all important parts of the incident, but that you have not included anything that doesn't develop your story.

...4. On a separate sheet of ruled paper, write the paragraph. Be sure to provide enough explanation about the various parts of the incident so that the reader doesn't have to "fill in the gaps."

Check the Answer Key on p. 108 before continuing.

EXERCISE F. *Plan and write a paragraph developed by reasons. Follow these steps, checking them off as you go.*

...1. Choose one of the following topics.
  a) Should One Always Tell the Truth?
  b) Industries That Pollute the Environment Should Be Shut Down
  c) The Importance of School Social Activities
  d) Why High School Boys Should (or Should Not) Play Football
  e) Should Homework be Eliminated?
  f) The Advantages (or Disadvantages) of Limiting Family Size by Law to Control Population Growth

...2. Using the chart below, plan your paragraph. Write a general statement of your opinion on the topic in the space provided. List specific *reasons* that support your general statement. If you have difficulty thinking of reasons, read the topic sentence to yourself and then ask the question "why?"

GS . . . .

. . . .

Type of Specifics . . . .

SP . . . .

SP . . . .

SP . . . .

SP . . . .

. . . 3. After you have listed your reasons, check them to make sure that all are directly related to the topic sentence.

. . . 4. On a separate sheet of ruled paper, write the paragraph. You'll probably need to explain each reason with several sentences of specific details. Also, provide any necessary connecting information.

. . . 5. Check your paragraph for errors in grammar, punctuation, and spelling. Then underline the topic sentence (and clincher, if there is one) and number the reasons as they appear in the paragraph.

Check the Answer Key on p. 108 before continuing.

step 18

Using Other Types and Combinations of Specifics

In addition to the four basic types of specifics (examples, facts, reasons, incident), there are some other types that are used less often.

Comparison or Contrast.   Pointing out similarities and differences, comparing an idea or thing with something that it resembles, contrasting an idea or thing with something that it differs from.

Analysis.   Breaking an idea or thing into its logical parts.

Steps in a Process.   A special kind of analysis, especially useful when giving instructions.

Descriptive Details.   Expressing how something looks, smells, feels, sounds, or tastes in such a way as to communicate the sensation to the reader.

Definition.   Explaining the meaning of an important term.

Quotation.   Repeating word for word what a knowledgeable person has said in support of your generalization. (Of course you must always give written credit to your source when quoting.)

Up to this point we've talked as though only one type of specifics could be used in any one paragraph. This is, of course, not always true. In fact, a good paragraph usually contains several types of specifics, even though one type may be used more than others. You are therefore free to use as many types of specifics as you feel are needed to logically support your general statement. It is helpful to keep in mind, though, what main types you are using.

Imagine that the general statements listed below are topic sentences of paragraphs. After each one write the type or types of specifics that you think would best *support that topic sentence. (Use mainly the basic four—reasons, facts, incident, examples—but include any of the other six—comparison/contrast, analysis, steps, description, definition, quotation—whenever you feel they are helpful.)*

1.   My life is based on certain principles and I attempt to live by them each day.

     Type(s) of Specifics . . . .

2.   While in many ways I am eager to be independent, there are some decisions that I would rather not have to make for myself.

     Type(s) of Specifics . . . .

3. If I were principal of this school, I would make some radical changes.

   Type(s) of Specifics . . . .

4. I simply cannot stand the type of person who thinks he knows everything.

   Type(s) of Specifics . . . .

5. It is really quite simple to change a tire once you know how.

   Type(s) of Specifics . . . .

6. As strange as it may sound, I've learned many things about myself by reading books.

   Type(s) of Specifics . . . .

7. Student government at our school is a failure.

   Type(s) of Specifics . . . .

8. The way I have been raised by my parents has influenced my personality tremendously.

   Type(s) of Specifics . . . .

9. The Grand Canyon was the most beautiful spot we visited on our vacation.

   Type(s) of Specifics . . . .

10. What does it mean to be a "good citizen?"

    Type(s) of Specifics . . . .

11. Conservation is essential if we are to save our natural resources.

    Type(s) of Specifics . . . .

12. Girls are well-known for talking too long on the telephone.

    Type(s) of Specifics . . . .

Check the Answer Key on p. 109 before continuing.

step 19   Ordering Specifics

The reader will find your paragraph much easier to follow if you arrange your specific details in a logical order, rather than writing them down in whatever random way they first occurred to you. Look over your list of specifics *before* you begin to write your paragraph and decide what is the most logical order of presentation. Some examples of the most important types of order follow.

Order of Time or Sequence. The specifics below are listed in *time* order: from first to last, from beginning to end, from earliest to latest.

GS   When I wash my car I like to do it properly.

SP   First, I gather all the clean rags and sponges, soap, water, and other equipment.

SP   Then, I make sure all windows are rolled up tight.

SP   Next, I proceed to wet and soap down all parts of the car.

SP   Finally, I rinse the entire car very thoroughly.

Order of Importance. The specifics below build in importance from least to most important. It is equally possible to go from most to least; what is essential is that there be a definite pattern in one direction or the other.

GS   Three qualities characterize a good citizen.

SP   Of course, every good citizen should be well informed about current events.

SP   In addition, a good citizen obeys all the laws and respects the government.

SP   But perhaps of greatest significance is the good citizen's willingness to use his right to vote and his right to participate fully in the governing process.

Order Necessary to Show Contrast or Comparison. When your general statement contains an obvious comparison, the supporting specifics may be ordered in one of two ways.

a)   1X, 2X, 3X, then 1Y, 2Y, 3Y

This order is shown in the example below, where all specifics about dogs are placed first, followed by comparable specifics about cats, presented in the same order.

GS   Cats make better pets than dogs.

SP   Dogs are messy, do not clean up after themselves. (1X)
SP   Dogs eat too much food, require too much care. (2X)
SP   Dogs jump up on people, knock over furniture. (3X)
SP   Cats, on the other hand, are clean and tidy. (1Y)
SP   Cats eat sparingly, take care of themselves. (2Y)
SP   Cats are usually well mannered, behave themselves. (3Y)

b) 1X/1Y, 2X/2Y, 3X/3Y

This second pattern for comparison arranges the two groups of specifics in alternation, as shown in the following example.

GS   Cats make better pets than dogs.

SP   Dogs are messy, do not clean up after themselves. (1X)
SP   Cats, on the other hand, are clean and tidy. (1Y)
SP   Dogs eat too much, require too much care. (2X)
SP   Cats, however, eat sparingly, take care of themselves. (2Y)
SP   Dogs jump up on people, knock over furniture. (3X)
SP   But cats are usually well mannered, behave themselves. (3Y)

EXERCISE A. *Identify which order of specifics was used to arrange the details in each of the paragraphs below. (If the order is contrast, indicate whether it is type a or type b.)*

1.   Every high school student should learn to type because of the many advantages typing has over script. First, typing is much less fatiguing than writing, especially when you use an electric typewriter. You can typewrite for hours without fatigue, while steady writing for a time will soon tire your hands. Second, no matter how tired you become, the character of typed letters never changes. On the other hand, script will tend to become sloppy after long periods of writing. Next, typing is always legible with a minimum of effort. At times personal script is so poor that it is difficult, if not impossible, to read. Legibility can contribute to an improved grade, since a teacher is more likely to give a low grade to a sloppily written paper than to a neat, typewritten one. Another advantage is speed. A good typist can type from forty to seventy words per minute, while he can write only about twenty to thirty words per minute by hand.

Order of Specifics . . . .

2.   My greatest disappointment, I think, was the time I went to camp in Vermont. When I first got there it was dark and I

couldn't see too much, but what I did see wasn't very promising—a small cabin with no windows and half a door which let in all the cold air every night. I had to sleep with six blankets! In the morning I walked down to the stables. The picture of the stables in the pamphlet I had received showed them bright and new. It must have been taken twenty or more years ago because, in reality, they were run-down and badly in need of paint. After that I walked up to the so-called lake, which was really a dirty pond with a cement bottom. Again, the pamphlet had been misleading. The next day I found out that there wasn't going to be as much horseback riding as the pamphlet had implied, and the promise of a lot of riding was what had decided me on the camp. Perhaps my experience would have been less disappointing to me had I been able to see what the camp was really going to be like before I arrived.

Order of Specifics . . . .

3. Women's fashions tend to change more rapidly and radically than men's. In the early 1900's, all women wore their skirts down to the ankle. Today, skirt length varies from floor-length to ten inches above the knee. Women's shoes have also gone through all sorts of changes in the last seventy years. For example, boots for women were very common around the turn of the century. Then, for years, they were not considered fashionable. Today they're back in style again in all colors, lengths, and materials. In fact, today's woman can wear all types of clothes—even slacks and shorts—on almost any occasion. While all of these changes were taking place in women's fashions, men's clothing remained pretty much the same until a couple of years ago. And, in fact, most men still wear the traditional "suit"—jacket, shirt, tie, and slacks—though bright colors, patterns, and a variety in cut are now more common.

Order of Specifics . . . .

4. In order to become a cheerleader, one must fulfill a number of requirements. Of course a cheerleader should be a good citizen and a responsible person, for she must set an example for the rest of the school by faithfully attending all of the games and pep rallies, as well as other school activities. Also

important is a girl's appearance. She must look her best at all times, not only because it makes her more attractive, but because she is the school's representative. The next requirement is essential: pep. Pep is an important quality in any good cheerleader because she must get the crowd into the spirit of the game. But pep must be accompanied by skill in executing the various jumps, leaps, cartwheels, arm motions, and other acrobatic feats needed in cheerleading. Unless the cheerleader has this skill, simply having pep will not be enough. Finally, one qualification tops the list: a good, loud voice.

Order of Specifics . . . .

5. An electronic computer, while able to perform certain mathematical calculations more quickly than man's brain, does not have the brain's complex structure. While a human brain consists of trillions upon trillions of nerve cells, a so-called "electronic brain" contains only about ten million electronic components. A human has the ability to create, to exercise initiative, to deduct, to reach conclusions, to doubt, to reason logically. A computer can only compute; it can multiply, divide, add, subtract, and perhaps extract roots. Also it must be carefully "programmed" in order to arrive at an answer; that is, it must be told in advance all the steps necessary to perform a particular operation. A man, however, can be given a problem and go on to solve it with no further instruction. Most of the time taken up by a computer for problem solving is in locating the appropriate steps and intermediate values stored in its massive memory banks. The human brain, on the other hand, uses most of its time in actual computations. In short, a human brain is vastly more complex and versatile than that of a computer and therefore far superior.

Order of Specifics . . . .

6. You should never smoke in bed because the consequences can be drastic. My neighbor, Mrs. Smith, found this out the hard way a couple of weeks ago. Coming home late from work and extremely tired, she fell onto the couch as soon as she entered her house. After an hour or so, she got up the energy to fix herself some dinner. Then, still feeling weary,

she took a warm bath and went to bed with a book. Soon afterward her troubles began. As she was reading, she lit a cigarette. Relaxed and comfortable, she began to doze over her book and, without realizing it, dropped her cigarette on the rug. A few minutes later she was fast asleep. Within an hour, smoke was rising from the rug, and moments later came the fire. When Mrs. Smith awoke, gasping for breath, she was horrified to find her bed in flames. Soon the fire department arrived and she was taken to the hospital with second degree burns. Catastrophes like this are common among people who smoke in bed.

Order of Specifics ....

7. Racial disturbances are the result of many different problems. One cause is bad housing. Often, the only place a racial minority can live is in a tenement among rats and roaches. Trash and garbage litter the streets, and whole families are cramped into two or three rooms, sometimes without windows or plumbing. There are usually no recreational areas in these ghettos, and children are forced to play in the streets as a result. Living in this type of environment has helped lead blacks, chicanos and other minorities into revolt. In addition, unemployment is high among these groups because of job discrimination. When people cannot find work by which to support their families, they fall into despair and dissatisfaction and a riot is easily ignited. But perhaps the most significant problem is inadequate education. For example, the schools in many black communities lack equipment, facilities, and qualified teachers. Because of this, students often become apathetic about obtaining an education and drop out. Even interested students are not given the proper training required for life in our highly competitive society, and despite hard work they find it difficult to secure jobs and create a stable family life. Poor education, then, is at the heart of the problem, but it is accompanied by poor housing and unemployment. Only the elimination of these problems will lessen the threat of minority violence.

Order of Specifics. ....

Check your answers on p. 109 before continuing.

In addition to the three main ways of ordering specifics—time, importance, contrast—there are several other logical orders which you may find useful.

Order of Familiarity. Moving from the known to the unknown, from what the reader is familiar with to what he is less familiar with.

Order of Difficulty. Moving from easy to hard.

Order of Complexity. Moving from simple to complex.

Order of Agreement. Starting with those parts of the topic that the reader is likely to agree with, and then moving on to the aspects that are more controversial or less likely to be accepted.

Order of Problem to Answer. Starting with a discussion of the problem or conflict, then moving to a presentation of the resolution or solution.

Order of Position. Moving logically from one place or location to another.

EXERCISE B. *Arrange the specifics in each list below in a logical order by numbering them 1, 2, 3, and so on. In the blank at the end of the list tell what order you used. You will probably use the three main orders—time, importance, contrast—most often, but feel free to use any of the other six when they seem more suitable. If you choose order of* contrast, *be sure to specify type* a *or type* b.

1. GS A person's education has a profound effect on his development.

   ... SP Elementary school gives the child an opportunity to develop basic skills, such as reading and writing, and to explore the natural world in which he lives.

   ... SP The chief influence of college is the specialized training in a vocational field, as well as the much broader exposure to new ideas and attitudes.

   ... SP Nursery school or kindergarten usually provides the child's first real chance to work and play with others his own age.

... SP In high school, the young person begins to understand himself as a unique individual and to develop many new interests and ideas outside his family circle.

Order of Specifics ....

2. GS Life in the city is considerably different from life in the suburbs.

... SP A person living in the city is close to many sources of entertainment.

... SP The streets of many suburban communities are lined with trees and shrubs and each house has its own grassy yard.

... SP People living in the city are constantly exposed to the hustle and bustle of urban life.

... SP If city dwellers want to see trees and grass, they must go to one of the public parks.

... SP Life in the suburbs is generally quiet and casual and generally more low-key than that in the city.

... SP Frequently, people living in suburban areas must go into the city for entertainment.

Order of Specifics ....

3. GS Watching the crowd at a baseball game is sometimes more interesting than watching the game itself.

... SP Down two rows and to the right is a row of twenty cans of beer, toward which a hand moves drunkenly, depositing the twenty-first empty beside the others.

... SP His rhythmic chant of "Peanuts, here!" rises and falls in measured cadence.

... SP Behind them, obviously amused at their unselfconscious lovemaking, is a spectacled old man, whose matronly wife is yelling vehemently: "Strike 'im out!"

   ... SP As your eyes wander around the stadium, you become a witness to a fascinating portrait of humanity in action.

   ... SP It totters on the edge of the wall and falls at the feet of the refreshment vendor.

   ... SP Further down the row is a young couple necking passionately, oblivious to what is happening on the diamond.

Order of Specifics ....

4. GS Playing the guitar well requires knowledge of several skills.

   ... SP Learning the fingerboard is also an elementary step.

   ... SP After having mastered these three basic skills, you are ready to move on to a more difficult skill: learning the chord positions.

   ... SP Still another is memorizing the finger positions of the notes.

   ... SP The technique for holding the pick, although apparently unimportant, is actually basic to playing the instrument.

Order of Specifics ....

5. GS Smoking in school isn't worth the risk of getting caught.

   ... SP He said that he smelled smoke in the room and wondered whether anyone had been smoking.

   ... SP One day I was smoking in the boy's restroom when a teacher walked in.

   ... SP Then he took me down to the principal's office where I was given a three-day suspension.

   ... SP He noticed them at about the same time and and asked me what was in my pocket, so I told him.

... SP   I furtively crushed my cigarette underfoot and was about to walk out when I noticed that the top of my cigarette pack was sticking out of my shirt pocket.

Order of Specifics ....

6. GS   The major problem with most programmed instruction used in schools today is that it tends to bore the student.

.... SP   Another possible solution is keeping the student motivated by using subject matter that he is interested in and that is pertinent to his daily life, or by supplementing the text with regular class-work that provides the motivation for him.

... SP   However, in taking these steps the student becomes bored, because the questions are so numerous and so much alike.

... SP   It is written in small steps to enable the student to make progress by taking small jumps in knowledge that he is sure to comprehend rather than giant leaps in which he might lose the trail.

... SP   This would give the student a chance to really grapple with the problem and understand it, rather than just plowing through question after question.

... SP   One method of reducing boredom might be to reduce the overall number of questions while increasing their difficulty.

Order of Specifics ....

Check your answers on p. 109 before continuing.

EXERCISE C. *Plan and write three paragraphs, using a different order of specifics for each. Choose three different topics from the list below that will allow you to use differing orders of details easily.*

    a)   The Stupidity of Some School Rules
    b)   How to Improve Your Vocabulary

c)   Learning to Drive
d)   If I Had Only Three Days to Live
e)   How to Shop Wisely
f)   Football Versus Rugby (or Soccer)
g)   Compact Cars Versus Larger Cars
h)   Two Characters from Short Stories (or Novels)
i)   Why I Would (or Would Not) Want to Live Forever
j)   Today's Youth
k)   Discrimination Is Far from Dead
l)   Why Men Are Superior (or Inferior) to Women
m)   Life in the City Versus Life on a Farm

Using the charts below, plan each of your three paragraphs as follows: Write a general statement about your topic. Next, write in the blank provided the type or types of specifics you think would be appropriate for supporting the general statement. Then, list the specifics, decide what order they should be presented in, and write the type in the blank provided. Finally, number your specifics accordingly.

GS . . . .

. . . .

Type(s) of Specifics . . . .

SP . . . .

SP . . . .

SP . . . .

SP . . . .

Order of Specifics . . . .

GS . . . .

. . . .

Type(s) of Specifics . . . .

SP . . . .

SP . . . .

SP . . . .

SP ....

Order of Specifics ....

GS ....

....

Type(s) of Specifics ....

SP ....

SP ....

SP ....

SP ....

Order of Specifics ....

Check the Answer Key on p. 109 before continuing.

step 20   Adding Signal Words

In attempting to make clear the relationships among the ideas in your paragraph, you will find it helpful to insert a special type of expression. You might think of such expressions as *signal words*, since they give the reader a signal as to what kind of idea is coming. For instance, if the next idea contradicts or modifies the previous one, an appropriate signal between them would be *but* or *however*. If the next idea is another in a series of reasons, a good signal would be *in addition* or *furthermore*. Such words help to explain the relationship between ideas and to connect specifics. They are essential to the clarity of your paragraphs. These signal words generally fall into five different categories.

Signals of Time.   next, soon, then, later, finally, after, first, second, *etc.*

Signal of Contrast.   but, however, on the other hand, nevertheless, otherwise, yet, *etc.*

Signals of Listing or Sequence. in addition, also, furthermore, moreover, another, likewise, similarly, next, finally, besides, first, second, *etc.*

Signals of Results. therefore, hence, thus, consequently, as a result, for, *etc.*

Signals of Examples. for instance, an example of this, for example, take the case of, *etc.*

EXERCISE A. *Letter (a, b, c, etc.) the signal words sequentially as they appear in each of the following paragraphs. Then, in the appropriate space provided below, tell what* kind *of signal word each is.*

1. Being fat is not quite as bad as it seems. Cute overweight girls have more to admire when they look into mirrors. When they find a nice dress, there is more of it to look nice in. In addition, it is economical to be corpulent; because it costs the same for a size 18 as it does for a size 10, fat girls certainly get more for their money. Furthermore, a pleasingly plump lassie never has to be afraid of being called "Twiggy." Besides, in the case of a great famine as the result of the expanding population, tubby girls will live longer than thinner members of their sex. In old age, overweight girls will never have to find outside hobbies to fill up their time, for they will be constantly occupied with grocery shopping and letting out seams in their clothes. Finally, fat girls have one last fringe benefit: there is more of them for their boy friends to love. Therefore, don't count your calories girls. Let it all hang out!

    a) . . . .   d) . . . .

    b) . . . .   e) . . . .

    c) . . . .

2. Every high school student should learn to type because of the many advantages that typing has over script. First, typing is much less fatiguing than writing. This is especially true in the case of electric typewriters. You can typewrite for hours without fatigue, while a long period of steady writing will tire your hands. Second, no matter how tired you

become, the character of typed letters never changes. Script, on the other hand, tends to get sloppy after long periods of writing. Next, typing is always legible with a minimum of effort. At times personal script is so poor that it is difficult, if not impossible, to read. Legibility can contribute to an improved grade, since a teacher is more likely to give a low grade to a sloppily written paper than to a neat, typewritten one. The biggest advantage, however, is speed. A good typist can type from forty to seventy words per minute while he can write only about twenty to thirty words per minute by hand.

a) ....   d) ....

b) ....   e) ....

c) ....

3. Though smoking is detrimental to health, many people do it anyway. Every individual has his own reasons for smoking. For instance, an adolescent may smoke for the sheer excitement of doing something different and forbidden. As he approaches adulthood, the teenager wants to try what adults are doing. Thus, part of smoking as a teen is the feeling that one has actually matured to the adult stage and has taken a step in life. Along with feeling that he has developed into a young adult, smoking tends to make a teenager feel "cool." Most adults, on the other hand, smoke from habit—developed in youth. For example, if a person takes up smoking in his adolescent years, it is likely he will continue to smoke throughout adulthood. People who smoke constantly rationalize their habit by saying it creates a relaxed feeling and eases their nerves. The reasons for smoking vary from a teen's curiosity to an adult's habit.

a) ....   c) ....

b) ....   d) ....

Check your answers on p. 109 before continuing.

EXERCISE B. *Turn back to the paragraphs you wrote for* step 19, Exercise C. *Insert any signal words you feel would help make the paragraph clearer and easier to read.*

EXERCISE C. *Write a paragraph according to the following steps, checking them off as you complete them.*

...1. Choose one of the following topics.
 a. The Kind of Life I Want at Age Seventy-five
 b. What to Do in Case of a Fire at Home
 c. A Book I Did Not Like
 d. Why I Like Sundays (or Sundaes)
 e. The Nature of My Daydreams

...2. Using the following chart, plan your paragraph. Write a general statement about your topic in the blank provided. Then fill in the type or types of specifics that will best support this topic sentence (see *steps 17-18*). List the supporting specifics. Decide what type of ordering would be most logical. Write which type you plan to use in the space provided (see *step 19*) and number your specifics in that order.

GS . . . .

. . . .

Type(s) of Specifics . . . .

SP . . . .

SP . . . .

SP . . . .

Order of Specifics . . . .

Check the Answer Key on p. 110 before continuing.

step 21   Adding Other Connectors

In addition to signal words, there are several other means of connecting the specifics in your paragraph. Here are three of the most useful.

1. Using pronouns which refer to words in preceding sentences. In the following example, "He" refers to "Terry" and "one" refers to "pencil." Such reference, through the use of a pronoun, helps to tie the two sentences together smoothly.

> I handed a pencil to Terry, the boy who sits behind me in math class. He had forgotten to bring one and was desperate because a test had been announced.

2. Using demonstrative adjectives (*this, that, those, these, such,* etc.) which refer to earlier words or ideas. In the following example, "This" refers to "shy" in the preceding sentence and helps to connect the two sentences.

> Bill Treadway had always been very shy. This shyness kept him from enjoying social activities.

3. Using a word or phrase that has the same meaning or relates to the same thing as a word or phrase in a preceding sentence. In the following example, "The little devil" refers to "Chris" and thus helps to link the two sentences.

> My little brother Chris is a holy terror. The little devil is constantly in trouble at school and is almost impossible to live with at home.

EXERCISE A. *For each sentence given below you have a choice of two sentences which could follow it. Circle the letter of the one which is best connected to the first sentence. Look for the various types of connecting devices discussed above, as well as for signal words. Underline the connector that caused you to make your choice.*

1. I enjoy reading science fiction stories.
   a) *R is for Rocket* by Ray Bradbury was very exciting.
   b) For instance, I found Ray Bradbury's *R is for Rocket* very exciting.

2. Bill likes to travel very much.
   a) Perhaps Bill likes to travel because his father is an airplane pilot.
   b) Perhaps he likes it because his father is an airplane pilot.

3. Most girls are sensible about how much make-up they use.

a) But there are also those who think that the more they use, the better they look.

b) There are some girls who think that the more make-up they use, the better they look.

4. I forgot to bring the money for my bus ticket.

   a) I could not accompany my class on a field trip.

   b) Consequently, I could not accompany my class on a field trip.

5. Most high-school students feel free to talk to their counselors about problems they encounter in school.

   a) However, others feel uncomfortable talking to any adult representing the school administration.

   b) Therefore, others feel uncomfortable talking to any adult representing the school administration.

6. My father's way of punishing me when I was a child was to make me stand in the corner.

   a) Ever since that time, I have had a deathly fear of corners.

   b) I am deathly afraid of corners now.

7. Disrupting a class is not difficult. One method I use is to make wisecracks about what the teacher is saying.

   a) You can throw spitballs at the girl sitting in the front row.

   b) Another is to throw spitballs at the girl sitting in the front row.

Check your answers on p. 110 before continuing.

EXERCISE B. *Rewrite the second sentence in each pair below, providing any connecting devices and signal words that would improve the connection between the sentences. Underline your linking device in each sentence.*

1. Franklin Prins was once a well-known attorney. Franklin Prins practiced law in my home town for thirty-five years.

   . . . .

   . . . .

2. When washing a dog, you should first fill a large tub with

warm, soapy water. Find the dog and lure him into the tub.

. . . .

. . . .

3. In the novel, *Moby Dick*, Herman Melville uses many unusual devices to carry the story line through the book. Melville turns the novel into a play at several points.

. . . .

. . . .

4. In 1967, Great Britain devalued its unit of currency, the pound. Devaluing the pound had an effect on most of the countries in the Western World.

. . . .

. . . .

5. Going steady has many disadvantages. A disadvantage of going steady is that you are tied down to one boy or girl and have no opportunity to get to know anyone else.

. . . .

. . . .

6. In my opinion, John F. Kennedy was a great President. One of the things that made John F. Kennedy a great President was that he inspired the youth of this country.

. . . .

. . . .

7. Craig Breedlove had to risk danger in breaking the land speed record. Craig Breedlove had to place himself in a machine that could become a coffin traveling at 600 miles per hour at any moment.

. . . .

. . . .

8. At Hilton High School the students are allowed to smoke in the cafeteria during lunch hour. At Madison High the students are not allowed to smoke at all.

   . . . .

   . . . .

9. My sister Suzanne is a fine dancer. She sings very well.

   . . . .

   . . . .

10. The assistant principal of our school is a high school dropout and a former convict. The assistant principal is not qualified for the position he holds.

    . . . .

    . . . .

11. In composing a good essay you should first plan and order each paragraph in outline form. You are ready to begin writing.

    . . . .

    . . . .

Check the Answer Key on p. 110 before continuing.

EXERCISE C. *Write a paragraph, following these steps and checking them off as you go.*

...1. Choose one of the following topics.
   a)   Characteristics of a Good Class President
   b)   Causes of Student Rebellion
   c)   The Role of Religion in the Life of a Teenager
   d)   How I'd Spend $3000
   e)   The Career I Want
   f)   The People I Admire

...2. Using the chart below, plan your paragraph. Write a general statement on your topic in the space provided. Then write in the appropriate blank the type or types of specifics which would best support it. List the supporting specifics.

GS . . . .

. . . .

Type(s) of Specifics . . . .

SP . . . .

SP . . . .

SP . . . .

SP . . . .

Order of Specifics . . . .

. . . 3.   Eliminate unrelated specifics, if there are any. Add new ones that occur to you.

. . . 4.   Decide on the appropriate type of ordering for your specifics, then number your list of specifics in that order.

. . . 5.   Insert any signal words that would make the paragraph easier to follow.

. . . 6.   Write your paragraph on a separate sheet of ruled paper, inserting signal words given in the outline, plus any others that seem necessary.

. . . 7.   Check your paragraph for gaps or interruptions resulting from failure to explain ideas completely and provide proper connectors.

. . . 8.   Check for errors in grammar, punctuation, and spelling; underline the topic sentence and clincher; circle all signal words and connecting devices.

Check the Answer Key on p. 110 before continuing.

step 22   Proofreading the Paragraph

By now you've learned to plan and write a paragraph carefully so that it says what you mean clearly and completely. But the job of writing a good paragraph doesn't end there. One more very important step must be taken: checking for careless errors. You must examine what you have written to make sure it is the best you can do and to eliminate any mistakes you can spot. Two things are essential to good proofreading: checking to make sure that your ideas are clearly presented, and checking closely for specific errors you may have missed.

First, read your paragraph aloud in order to hear how it sounds. This will help you find gaps in your thought, ideas that are not explained adequately, careless omission of words, and obvious errors, in punctuation and grammar. If you're embarrassed at the thought of reading your own paper aloud, find a secluded spot, turn the radio up to drown out your mumbling, and read quietly to yourself. If you have no hesitation about reading aloud, it's often helpful to read to someone else—someone who can tell you if your paragraph "makes sense" and if you have any glaring mistakes.

Then, read (aloud or silently) the paper through again several times—looking for a different type of error with each reading. Except perhaps for those people who are trained in professional proofreading, it's not humanly possible to spot every error you may have made by reading your paragraph only once. You must read it a number of times in order to catch them all. Here is a list of the most common types of errors.

Poor Organization. Do you have a good topic sentence with supporting specifics? Do you need a clincher?

Unrelated Specifics. Do all of the specific details help explain or prove the topic sentence?

Poor Order of Specifics. Are your specifics arranged in some appropriate, logical pattern?

Signal Words.   Have you provided the proper signal and linking expressions to connect your ideas?

Errors in Grammar.   Are all your sentences complete? Have you improperly joined two sentences? Do subjects and verbs agree? Do pronouns and their antecedents agree? Are pronouns in the proper case?

Punctuation Errors.   Have you used commas where needed to set off or separate items? Have you avoided using unnecessary commas? Have you used apostrophes correctly? Have you been careful to use colons and semicolons properly? Have you avoided needless use of dashes?

Spelling Mistakes.   Have you checked the dictionary for the exact spelling of any word that you are not absolutely sure of?

Neatness.   Is your handwriting legible? Are your margins adequately wide and straight? Have you indented the first line of the paragraph?

After you have proofread your work, correcting errors and making improvements, recopy the paragraph before turning it in.

Proofread the paragraph below, which contains many of the errors outlined in this lesson. You should read the paragraph through once for each type of error. Correct the error in the paragraph itself by crossing it out and writing the correct form above it.

The student should first of all find a quiet well-lighted place with no detracting noises. The place they choose should be level and large enough for all the books, papers, and materials that they need. All these material's should be gathered before beginning to work. Since it is a waste of time to constantly have to stop and go running after a book or ruler. The time one chooses to study is important. Generally it should be at a time convient to the student, but it should not begin to late in the evening. Breaks in study time is very necessary; since one cannot be expected to consentrate for long periods without a rest. In fact, research studys show that ones study is more efficient if they work for about forty-five minutes and take a ten-minute snack break. One should be careful, though, that his "break" time does not exceed the amount of time he spends actually studying. Once the student has found the proper environment for their study and have established a time to begin, the real work starts. Studying is a complex process that requires consentration. If one has textbook assignments to read, this reading should be done actively; with an attempt to remember the main points of the assignment. Watching a serious television play also requires this same sort of active involvement. If one has lecture notes to review, he should do more than skim over them halfheartedly. The good student will be thinking of possible test questions based on these notes, by doing this, he is usually not totally surprised when he reads the examination questions. If one takes care to follow these steps when he studys—He will find that the effort pays off in better grades, and more free time.

Check your answers on p. 110 before continuing.

step 23   Trying It on Your Own

If you have worked all the steps preceding this one carefully, you will have learned how to write a good paragraph. Prove to yourself—and your teacher—that you can do it by writing a paragraph on one of the topics listed below. You should outline it on a separate sheet of ruled paper, according to the method you've learned before. Write a rough draft of the paragraph, proofread it, and then copy it over before submitting it to your teacher.

a) The Car I'd Like Most to Own
b) Decisions I Should Be Allowed to Make for Myself
c) The Fears I Live With
d) The Advantages (or Disadvantages) of Living in a Commune
e) Two Different Teachers
f) The Causes of Family Quarrels

step 24   Understanding the Essay

You're now ready to start planning and writing entire essays composed of several paragraphs. Essays are not really any more difficult to write than paragraphs, especially if you keep in mind one essential point: *An essay is simply an enlargement of a paragraph.*

The essay and the paragraph comprise the same elements—general statement, specifics, order of details, signal words and connectors, clincher, and all the rest. It's as if the structure of a paragraph were put under a photographic enlarger and expanded into a bigger version. Every element of the paragraph is in the essay—and in the same proportion.

The *topic sentence* (general statement) in a paragraph	becomes	the *thesis sentence* in the introductory paragraph of the essay.
The *supporting specifics* that explain the topic sentence	become	the main *supporting points* of the essay, each one of which is the *topic sentence* of the paragraph in which it is explained.
The *clincher* in a paragraph	becomes	the concluding paragraph of the essay.

Realizing that the essay is similar in its structure to the paragraph, let's look more closely at the parts of a good essay.

An Introductory Paragraph.   The first paragraph in the essay, which tells the reader what the essay is going to be about.

A Thesis Sentence.   One sentence, contained in the introduction, which gives the central idea or opinion that the essay will try to prove.

Paragraphs of Supporting Specifics.   One paragraph for each main supporting point. Each of these paragraphs is constructed just as you learned earlier.

A Conclusion.   One paragraph at the end summarizing the main points and/or restating the thesis sentence of the essay.

EXERCISE A.   *Read the essay below and mark it as follows.*

1.   Find the introductory paragraph and label it in the margin.

2.   Place a wavy line under the thesis sentence.

3.   Decide what three main supporting points are used to prove the thesis. Underline the topic sentences of the three paragraphs which explain each of these supporting points.

4.   Examine each of the supporting paragraphs. Number the specifics which support the topic sentence and put a double line under the clincher, if there is one. Circle the signal words and connecting devices.

5.   Find the conclusion and label it in the margin.

Joining the Peace Corps

A person applying for the Peace Corps will find he has to go through a complex procedure. This includes meeting certain qualifications, responding to questionnaires and examinations, and going through a period of training.

There are several qualifications which an applicant must have. First, he must be at least eighteen years old and a citizen of the United States. He can be married, but if both he and his wife want to serve, they must have no children under the age of eighteen. A third qualification is vocational skill. This means that the applicant must already know how to do something like teach or farm, because the program has no provision for training him. However, neither a college education nor knowledge of a foreign language is required. Another qualifcation is that he must not have any serious physical, mental or emotional disturbances. Most important of all, though, he must be willing to work for two years.

If his qualifications meet Peace Corps standards, the applicant must provide various kinds of information. First, he must fill out a questionnaire, listing his skills, hobbies, how much education he has had and where, his special interests, and his work background, if any. The applicant must also provide references from friends, teachers, and/or employers. Furthermore, he must take placement tests—which are noncompetitive and test his aptitudes and ability to learn foreign languages. A volunteer is picked for training on the basis of the information he gives on the questionnaire, the aptitude and ability he shows on the tests, and his references.

After taking the tests, a chosen volunteer must go through a training period of eight to ten weeks at a United States college. During this time, the volunteer is taught a great deal about the country in which he will be working. He studies its language, history, and culture. He is also given technical, physical, and health training to enable him to remain healthy while living like the natives of the country where he will be working. Another important part of the training is learning about the history of the United States and the meaning of democracy. This enables the volunteer to explain our system of government to others when he is asked. When the period of training ends, final selections of volunteers are made.

After the final selections, the successful volunteer is sent to a foreign country, where he serves for two years. By the time these two years are completed, he understands that the initial selection and training process was worthwhile.

Check your answers on p. 111 before continuing.

EXERCISE B. *The following essay is somewhat more complex than the first one you examined, but has the same general structure. Read through the entire essay once, then go back and mark it as follows, checking off each step as you complete it.*

...1.   Find the introductory paragraph and label it in the margin.

...2.   Place a wavy line under the thesis sentence. Be sure you've chosen the proper one!

...3.   Decide what three main supporting points are used to prove the thesis. Underline the topic sentences of the paragraphs which explain each of these supporting points.

...4.   Number the specifics in each paragraph which support the topic sentence. (Don't confuse explanatory and connecting information with the main specifics.)

...5.   Circle the signal words and connecting devices throughout the essay.

...6.   Find the conclusion and label it in the margin.

Today's teenager encounters many problems in his diversified life. Nevertheless, few teenagers ever discuss their problems with their parents—the two people who love them most and want the best for them—but prefer to talk about them with friends. Most adults feel they are aware of their teenager's problems and readily available to help solve them. But the teenager often fails to bring his problems before his parents because he senses in them distrust, preoccupation, and a lack of understanding—all of which seem to be contributing factors in this unfortunate failure to communicate.

Many adolescents feel that an older person, such as a parent, is unable to relate to the problems of the present-day youth. Some parents fail to understand because of the different environment in which they grew up, which produced different experiences and problems. For example, most parents see "going steady" as undesirable, even though most teenagers do it. The reason they dislike this practice is that when they were young it meant the couple was planning to be engaged soon. Now, of course, this is not the case. Other parents tend to underestimate the pressures on today's students, such as the necessity of getting superior grades in high school. When they were ready to go to college, the main requirement was having enough money. Today, however, it is necessary for a student to be in the upper fifth of his class if he is to enter a competitive university. Such things may be extremely important to the teen, yet can seem merely foolish to an adult who does not realize the seriousness of the problem. Parents also fail to realize the change in life style their teenagers are making. They often cannot accept the fact that the dependent adolescent is changing into a self-reliant adult. Along with this change emerge added responsibilities and privileges. However, when giving advice, many a parent acts as though he were addressing a young child rather than someone who is almost an adult. Due to this lack of understanding on the parents' part, the teenager feels he has no choice but to turn to his friends, who have similar problems and are more apt to understand him. Simple misunderstandings then, such as those mentioned here, may become major stumbling blocks to attempts at communication between teenager and parent.

Distrust is another cause for this lack of communication. While parents may say they trust their teenagers, their actions often indicate otherwise. For example, many parents listen in on their children's phone calls or open their mail, because they do not trust them to behave themselves properly. Also, parents frequently impose unreasonable restrictions on the adolescent's activities, simply because they do not trust his judgment. No young person is going to talk openly to an adult who shows no faith in his intelligence or his actions. Furthermore, many parents demonstrate quite clearly that they are not deserving of trust themselves. It may be that they simply repeat to another person in the family something told to them in confidence, but to many teens this is an act of disloyalty. When this kind of mutual distrust develops, the lines of communication break down.

Another reason the teenager does not bring his problems to his parents is that they are often too busy or too wrapped up in their own lives to give him the attention he needs. To some parents, social commitments are more important than being at home to discuss the problems of their children. Or they feel that they can fulfill their responsibilities by giving their children money and a car. Some fathers, for example, are so busy working to provide these material comforts for their families that they have no time left to spend with their children. Even the television set can become an obstacle between parents and children. It is next to impossible for the teenager to bring his problems before his parents when they are sitting glued to the screen all evening every evening. Parents who are too involved with their own activities to notice their teenager's problem force him to seek advice elsewhere. In such families, lack of communication is due to the parents' selfishness.

Lack of communication between the generations will continue until adults realize that teenagers are maturing individuals who need attention, understanding, and respectful trust. Lack of any of these elements in the parents' attitude will always create barriers between teenager and parent. These barriers must be broken and conquered before meaningful communication can begin.

Check your answers on p. 112 before continuing.

EXERCISE C. *Fill in the chart below by selecting the appropriate items from the essay above. You may abbreviate if necessary.*

Thesis Sentence . . . .
. . . .
. . . .

First Main Point . . . .

    GS   (Topic Sentence) . . . .

    . . . .

    SP . . . . . : . . . .

    SP . . . .

    SP . . . .

Second Main Point . . . .

    GS   (Topic Sentence) . . . .

    . . . .

    SP . . . .

    SP . . . .

    SP . . . .

Third Main Point . . . .

    GS   (Topic Sentence) . . . .

    . . . .

    SP . . . .

    SP . . . . . . - . . . .

    SP . . . .

Check your answers on p. 114 before continuing.

step 25 — Formulating a Thesis

Like the topic sentence in a paragraph, the *thesis sentence* in an essay is a general statement indicating what is going to be discussed. A good thesis sentence has the following characteristics.

1. It's a complete sentence (not *Why boys are smarter than girls*, but *Boys are smarter than girls.*)

2. It's general enough to include all the specific details in the essay.

3. It indicates the writer's opinion—his point of view or attitude toward the subject. In other words, a good thesis is arguable or controversial. Hence, *Flowers are pretty* is not as good a thesis as *Flowers are more useful to science than most people realize.*

For each pair given below, circle the letter preceding the statement that is the better thesis. Keep in mind the requirements listed above.

1. a) There are fads in clothing.
   b) Clothing fads are often ridiculous.

2. a) Parent and child communication
   b) Parents and children cannot communicate.

3. a) The tricks used by advertisers to lure the public
   b) Advertisers use many tricks to get the public to buy their products.

4. a) Despite the grumbling of most students, homework is an important part of the learning process.
   b) Should homework be eliminated?

5. a) The pro's and con's of capital punishment are continually debated.
   b) Capital punishment should be abolished.

6. a) Winter sports are invigorating, interesting, and fun.
    b) Why people should participate in winter sports

7. a) A workable definition of "independence" is needed.
    b) What do we mean by "independence"?

8. a) The architect contributes much to modern America.
    b) The contribution of the architect to modern America

9. a) An examination of the problems of today's teenagers
    b) The problems of today's teenagers are underestimated by most adults.

10. a) The United States Post Office should be sold to a private corporation.
    b) Increasing the efficiency of the United States Post Office by selling it to a private corporation

Check your answers on p. 115 before continuing.

step 26   Planning the Essay

There are several basic steps you should go through in planning your essay *before* you begin to write. Since the structure of an essay is so similar to that of a paragraph, this planning parallels very closely the planning of a good paragraph.

1. Write the thesis sentence. Make sure it's specific enough to say exactly what you're going to write about, but general enough to allow you to include adequate supporting details. Your thesis must show your position on the topic. Take a point of view; don't just write "about" something. Nonetheless, your thesis should not be stated in terms of you, the writer (*In this essay I shall attempt to prove that taxes are unnecessarily high*). Instead, simply state your opinion or position directly (*Taxes are unnecessarily high*).

2. Jot down the main ideas that support the thesis. Think about your thesis. Ask yourself "why?" Decide what ideas prove or

explain the thesis. Combine those that are similar. Eliminate any that are not directly related to your thesis or do not really add support to your argument. You should end up with three or four main supporting points.

3. Prepare an outline. This outline should consist of
   a) Thesis sentence
   b) Main points listed in a logical order. (See *step 19*; this information applies to the main points of the essay as well as to those of the paragraph.)
   c) Paragraph outline for each main point. (You will usually devote one paragraph to each supporting point. Although you may find it appropriate to write more than one in some instances, the one-point/one-paragraph rule is helpful in the beginning.) Outline as follows.
      i) Write a topic sentence (your general statement).
      ii) Decide on the best kinds of supporting specifics.
      iii) List the specifics. Eliminate any not directly related to the topic sentence.
      iv) Decide on the most logical ordering of specifics.
      v) Number of specifics in the order which they will appear in the paragraph.
      vi) Add signal words where appropriate.
   d) Any needed signal words at the beginning of paragraphs to help the reader see the relationships among your main points (paragraphs). Add them to your outline before beginning to write.

Now let's see if you can apply these steps to your own writing. First, choose one of the following essay topics.
   a) Is Religion Dead in the Twentieth Century?
   b) What It Means to Be Mature
   c) The Changes I'd Like to Make in Myself
   d) The Case Against Capital Punishment
   e) The Perfect Community

Plan your essay by filling in the chart below. At this point you're simply to plan the essay. Do not write it in final form until you've worked through step 27. *Follow the steps given above in filling out the chart.*

Thesis Sentence . . . .

. . . .

First Main Point . . . .

   GS   (Topic Sentence) . . . .

. . . .

   Type(s) of Specifics . . . .

   SP . . . .

   SP . . . .

   SP . . . .

   SP . . . .

   Order of Specifics . . . .

Second Main Point . . . .

   GS   (Topic Sentence) . . . .

. . . .

   Type(s) of Specifics . . . .

   SP . . . .

   SP . . . .

   SP . . . .

   SP . . . .

   Order or Specifics . . . .

Third Main Point . . . .

   GS   (Topic Sentence) . . . .

. . . .

   Type(s) of Specifics . . . .

   SP . . . .

   SP . . . .

   SP . . . .

SP . . . .

Order of Specifics . . . .

Check the Answer Key on p. 115 before continuing.

step 27   Writing the Essay

Turn your outline (*step 26*) into a complete essay as follows, checking each step off as you go.

...1. Write an introductory paragraph containing the thesis sentence. Your first paragraph should provide an introduction to the central idea of your paper. Don't just plunge into your first main point. Instead, give the reader any background information that he might need, explain why your topic is important to him, tell him what point you're setting out to prove (your thesis), and give him a clue to how you plan to prove it. Not every introduction will include all of these things, but each must contain at least the thesis sentence. (See the introductory paragraph of *Parent-Child Communication Problems*, p. 75, for an example of a good introduction.)

...2. Write a paragraph for each of the main supporting points, following the paragraph outlines you prepared as part of the essay outline for *step 26*. Each of these supporting paragraphs should be organized in the same manner as the paragraphs you wrote earlier. (The introductory paragraph generally does not follow the standard pattern. It is a special-purpose paragraph and has a pattern of its own which we will discuss in *step 28*.)

...3. Write a concluding paragraph to summarize your supporting ideas and restate your thesis.

...4. After you've completed your essay, mark it as follows.
a) Put a wavy line under the thesis sentence.
b) Underline topic sentences of supporting paragraphs.

c) Number the specifics in each supporting paragraph.

d) Circle signal words in your paragraphs.

(Of course, these four steps are simply to help you visualize the structure of your essay and usually would not be included in an essay turned in to your teacher.)

Check the Answer Key on p. 115 before continuing.

step 28   Building Better Introductions

As we mentioned in *step 27*, the introduction is a special-purpose paragraph which orients your reader to the topic and tells him what you are trying to prove. It should attract the reader's attention and lead him into the essay. It often defines important terms, gives necessary background information, and previews the main points of the essay. And, of course, it *always* contains that *thesis sentence*—the statement of what it is the essay will attempt to prove. In this lesson we will look at two useful forms of the introduction.

Funnel Introduction. This is one of the simplest introductions, so named because it begins with a very broad general idea and continues with more and more specific ideas until it arrives at the thesis sentence—the most specific idea in the introductory paragraph. On the following page is an example of the *funnel* introduction, set up in the shape of a triangle to illustrate how it moves from the most general, through succeedingly more specific ideas, to a statement of the thesis. Notice how this introductory paragraph starts with a very general idea ("The life of a teenager in modern America is not always pleasant"). Then it moves to a more specific aspect of that idea (his "conflicts and problems"). The next idea ("Most of these problems center around school") is still more specific. The final statement ("The primary problem created by school is the intense pressure for good grades.") is the thesis and is the most specific sentence in the paragraph. (Again, remember that the introduction is a special kind of paragraph and does not follow the usual structure of general statement supported by specifics.)

The life of a teenager in modern America is not always pleasant. He is faced
with a multitude of conflicts and problems, many of which seem almost
impossible to overcome. Most of these problems center around
school, not at all surprising considering that the teenager
devotes an average of eight hours a day to school
and school-related activities. The primary
problem created by school
is the intense pres-
sure for good
grades.

EXERCISE A. *Try writing a funnel introduction to the essay you wrote for* step 27. *Start with the most general idea you can think of that is related to your thesis. Get progressively more specific (at least two more steps) until you arrive at the thesis. (If you have trouble understanding how to write sentences that become progressively more specific, review* step 3.)

Check the Answer Key on p. 115 before continuing.

Contrast Introduction. This is another type of introduction that's easy to write and is especially appropriate when your thesis contradicts or modifies a commonly held belief or assumption. For example, if your thesis sentence is "It is more difficult to learn to ski than most people realize," you could write an introduction such as this.

Most people assume that learning to ski is not extremely difficult. They imagine the process consists of little more than strapping on two long boards, pushing off at the top of a hill, and gliding gracefully and effortlessly to the bottom. However, learning to ski is more difficult than these people realize, and requires long hours of practice, extremely good physical condition, and a lot of determination.

Notice that the *contrast* introduction starts off with a discussion of some commonly held belief or assumption. This assumption is explained in detail and then the thesis, the opposite of this assumption, is presented at the end of the introduction. Here is another example of the *contrast* introduction.

> To a great many adults, a teenager is typically a shiftless, lazy, irresponsible kid, who cares about nothing but his own selfish interests and who never gets his hair cut or takes a bath. These adults see the average young person as a spoiled brat who resents authority and stays out late at night drag racing. However, these adults are badly mistaken. The typical teenager is not only intelligent and enthusiastic, but he also has a keen sense of responsibility and eagerness to help others. (*Thesis sentence underlined.*)

EXERCISE B. *Using the thesis sentence you wrote for* step 27, *write a* contrast *introduction similar to the examples given above. First ask yourself what commonly held belief or idea your thesis contradicts. Start your introduction with a presentation of this assumption, explain it in some detail (a couple of sentences), and then, after a signal of contradiction (*however, on the other hand, but, *etc.*), present your thesis. Write your introduction on a separate sheet of ruled paper.*

Check the Answer Key on p. 115 before continuing.

A good introduction often contains a *preview* of the main points that are going to be used to support the thesis. The writer gives the reader a sort of "map of the landscape" or hint of the organization of the essay to make it easier for him to follow. The preview can come either before or after the thesis sentence and should be worked into the introduction very subtly. Avoid such obvious and awkward statements as *I shall prove this thesis by showing that*.... Here is an introduction based on the *funnel* example above, but with a preview of the supporting points added.

> The life of a teenager in modern America is not always pleasant. He is faced with a multitude of conflicts and problems, many of which seem almost impossible to overcome. Most of these problems center around school, not at all surprising considering that the teenager devotes an average of eight hours a day to school and school-related activities. The primary problem created by school is the intense pressure for good grades. In some cases the teenager is expected by his parents to do well in order to get into college. In others, teachers are the ones who create the pressure, by setting standards that are too high for the average student. And sometimes the pressure comes from the teen himself.

You will remember that the thesis sentence is "The primary problem created by school is the intense pressure for good grades." Notice that following the thesis are three causes of this problem. These are the three main points, or *factors*, of the thesis that will be used to prove or explain it. Introducing them in the opening paragraph gives the reader a hint of how the paper will be organized. Given this preview you would expect that the writer of the essay will devote one supporting paragraph to *parents*, another to *teachers*, and a third to *the teen himself*.

EXERCISE C. *In each of the introductory paragraphs below, underline the thesis sentence. Then indicate in the blank which construction (*funnel *or* contrast*) was used. Finally, number the factors in the* preview *of main supporting points.*

1.   Many parents complain that their teenagers do not come to them with their problems. These adults think that their children are attempting to keep them "in the dark" about their activities. Assuming that the teen has some suspicious reasons for not coming to them with his problem, parents blame him for the lack of communication that results. However, the fault for the teen's hesitancy to discuss his problems openly with his parents often lies entirely with the adults, because of their lack of understanding, their automatic distrust, and their constant preoccupation with other activities.

Type of Introduction . . . .

2.   Too often parents think the way to rear a child is to give him guidance in the proper way to think and act. This "guidance" too often becomes an actual molding of his personality to suit the parent, as is seen in parental lectures beginning with the old clichès, "if I were you I would. . . ." or "When I was your age I. . . ." These parents, while they may have the good of the child at heart, are nevertheless making a grave mistake by trying to compel him to act or think in certain ways. What the teen needs instead is a type of love which gives him the freedom and confidence to develop his own opinions in matters such as religion, morality, and choice of friends.

Type of Introduction . . . .

3. School is a complex mixture of academic and extracurricular activities. Although the academic side is perhaps the most essential, extracurricular activities often give the student important opportunities for developing a sense of responsibility and increasing his ability to work with others. The student can find such opportunities in an athletic program. A sport such as basketball helps young people stay physically fit, while at the same it makes them more responsible and better able to function in a group.

Type of Introduction ....

4. The prevailing attitude in America today is that everyone should get a college degree. This may be the result of the difficulties many members of the older generation have encountered in getting ahead without one. Or it may be caused by the tremendous increase in knowledge and the general opinion that it is necessary to keep abreast of new developments in science and technology. In any case, our colleges and universities are fast becoming overcrowded, and high school students are finding themselves under increasing pressure to earn good grades. But what about the young man who wants nothing more than to become a good auto mechanic? Or what about the girl whose goal is to get married and be a good mother? Or what about the young man who plans a career in military service? In each of these cases, a college education, while it might be helpful, is not essential, and the student should be encouraged to prepare himself for some other type of special training.

Type of Introduction ....

Check your answers on p. 115 before continuing.

step 29   Providing Transitions

Just as it is necessary to add signal words and connecting devices between the specifics in a paragraph, it is also necessary to provide them between the paragraphs in an essay. These links are basically of the same types as those found within paragraphs.

1. Signal words at the beginning of a paragraph to show its relationship to the preceding paragraph (see *step 20*).

2. Pronouns which refer to nouns in the preceding paragraph.

3. Demonstrative adjectives (*this, that,* etc.) referring to ideas in the preceding paragraph.

4. Repetition of key words or ideas from the last sentence of the preceding paragraph.

5. Reference to the main idea in a preceding paragraph.

Devices such as these provide a *transition,* or smooth movement from one paragraph to the next, helping to eliminate awkward and abrupt interruptions in the flow of ideas. In your essay outline, include any transitional devices you think are needed between paragraphs. Then, when you write the essay, you can readily supply them to keep your ideas moving smoothly.

EXERCISE A. *In each group below you are given a sentence that you're to imagine is the last sentence in a paragraph, and two sentences from which to choose the first sentence of the next paragraph. Circle the letter of the sentence in each group that provides the smoothest transition. Underline the transitional or connecting devices.*

1. A simple misunderstanding, then, can become a major stumbling block to communication between teenager and parent.
   a) Embarrassment plays a considerable part in the lack of communication between generations.
   b) Embarrassment also plays a considerable part in this lack of communication between generations.

2. Reading a textbook assignment actively, therefore, is an excellent way to use your study time most effectively.
   a) Another effective study habit is that of raising the right questions as you read.
   b) You should learn to raise the right questions as you read.

3. Courses at the high school level are generally difficult, and the student is often expected to work on his own.
   a) On the other hand, the junior high program is organized quite differently.
   b) The junior high program is organized quite differently.

4. This preoccupation with the past reflects the emphasis in modern psychology on formation of behavior patterns during early childhood.
   a) Despite the obvious importance of the past, however, the sensitive reader sees a deeper meaning in the novel.
   b) The sensitive reader sees a deeper meaning in the novel.

5. But, in general, the student who is interested in school takes a more active role in school affairs than the apathetic student—by running for offices, working hard on committees, helping make to plans and formulate ideas, and interacting with administrators and teachers.
   a) As a result of this more active role, the interested student develops faster socially.
   b) The interested student often develops faster socially.

6. The third basic pattern is order of importance, a method of organization in which the details are placed in ascending or descending order, according to how important they are to the argument.
   a) Any two or three of these orders can appear in the same paragraph, but usually one predominates.
   b) Often two or three orders can appear in the same paragraph, but usually one predominates.

7. Thus, the natives of Africa accepted the domination of the white man for many years, apparently without question or regret.
   a) But they will no longer accept such domination passively.
   b) The natives will no longer accept domination passively.

8. And finally, tie shoes give the foot more support and are therefore more healthful.
   a) Slip-on shoes, generally called "loafers," are more popular.

b) Nevertheless, slip-on shoes, generally called "loafers," are more popular.

9. These Greek myths, therefore, have much in common with the Biblical story of the creation.
   a) Likewise, both Greek mythology and the Bible contain stories of a great flood in which all but a few people were destroyed.
   b) The story of a great flood in which all but a few people were destroyed can be found in both Greek mythology and in the Bible.

10. The materials were assembled and I was ready to begin work immediately.
    a) I attacked the Spanish translation, which I dreaded the most.
    b) First, I attacked the Spanish translation, which I dreaded the most.

Check your answers on p. 116 before continuing.

EXERCISE B. *Look over the essay you wrote in* step 27. *Determine whether the ideas flow smoothly from one paragraph to the next. Are the relationships between the paragraphs made clear? Add any connecting devices that are needed.*

step 30   Learning to Conclude

Some students consider the concluding paragraph to be the most troublesome in the essay. Writing a conclusion should not be difficult for you if you keep the following points in mind.

1. Your conclusion can be a summary of the main points of your essay (stated in different words, of course, than when they appeared earlier) along with a restatement of your thesis (again in different words).

2. Your conclusion will be smoother if you relate it in some

way to the last supporting paragraph by repeating an appropriate key word or idea.

3. If your reader needs to see the relevance of your idea to his own life or to the world in general, your conclusion might point this out.

4. Sometimes the reader comes to the end of an essay asking "so what?" In that case, the concluding paragraph needs to clarify the significance of the thesis.

5. Try constructing a conclusion that is an "upside-down funnel"; that is, start with a restatement of the thesis and then enlarge the idea with statements that become more and more general to show the setting which gives the idea its significance.

6. If your paper is short and you feel that a conclusion would sound "tacked on," solve the problem by writing an extended clincher for the last supporting paragraph, in which you "echo" the thesis statement.

Look again at the essay you wrote for step 27. *Write a better conclusion for it by following some of the suggestions listed above.*

Check the Answer Key on p. 116 before continuing.

step 31   Proofreading the Essay

Your essay is not finished until you have proofread it carefully, corrected your errors, and recopied it. Proofreading an essay is exactly like proofreading a paragraph (see *step 22*), but for the sake of clarity, let's review the process.

Read the entire essay aloud in order to hear what it sounds like. Listen for gaps in your thoughts, ideas that are not explained adequately, careless omission of words, and obvious mistakes in punctuation and grammar. You might also ask someone else to listen to you or to read the essay as well, looking for mistakes you've missed and making suggestions for improvement. Then read the paper through again several times—looking closely for a different type of error with each reading. Here are the most important types to watch out for.

Poor Organization.   Does your paper have a precise central idea (thesis) stated in the introduction? Are the supporting points of this thesis given in logical order? Does your paragraphing indicate these logical divisions?

Unrelated Specifics.   Do all the main points relate directly to the thesis? Do all specifics in each paragraph help to prove or explain the topic sentence?

Lack of Order.   Are the main points arranged in an appropriate, logical pattern? Are the specifics within each paragraph arranged in a logical order?

Signal Words and Connectors.   Have you provided the proper signal words and linking devices to connect paragraphs, as well as to connect the specifics within each paragraph?

Errors in Grammar.   Are all your sentences complete? Have you improperly joined two sentences? Do subjects and verbs agree? Do pronouns and their antecedents agree? Are pronouns in the proper case?

Punctuation Errors.   Have you used commas where needed to set off or separate items? Have you avoided using unnecessary commas? Have you used apostrophes correctly? Have you been careful to use colons and semicolons properly? Have you avoided needless use of dashes?

Spelling Mistakes.   Have you checked the dictionary for the exact spelling of any words you're not absolutely sure of?

Neatness.   Is your handwriting legible? Are your margins adequately wide and straight? Have you indented the first line of each paragraph?

Cars I Would Not Want to Own

There are over a quarter of a million automobiles sold in the United States each year. Many types are available; foreign cars and American cars, convertables and sedans, big cars and little cars. This variety is the result of the wide range of tastes of the driving population. There is three kinds of cars which doesn't suit my taste at all, and which I would never own. One type is impractical, another is little and ugly, and a third is poorly made.

An example of an impractical car is the Excalibur SS, perhaps you have never seen one of these cars. It bears a strong resemblance to the Dusenberg of years ago or to an old MG, early 1951 or 1952. One of the things I don't like about it are that it only comes in a convertible model. That's fine in the summer or on a sunny day, but when it rains or when winter comes, its rather impractical. Winter is perhaps the roughest though. Mainly because the car is not even equipped with a heater. And the softtop has plastic side windows and a plastic rear window that leaks and yellows in the sun and becomes briddle with age. This car is fitted with a 327 cubic inch engine from the Corvette Stingray. The car does not weigh more than 2000 pounds, compared to the Corvette, which weighs approximately 3200 pounds this year. With over 350 horsepower and so little weight, the Excalibur is very dangerous, you can't come near controlling it on accelleration around curves or on a panic stop. Combining these shortcommings with a $10,000 price tag, you have a very impractical car.

A car that I wouldn't want is one of those ugly little foreign "bugs" you see everywhere. The Volkswagen is a good example, this simply isn't my idea of a car with good looks. In addition, its to small for safety. If you were hit in the side by a large car or by a truck, you'd be finished. You also can't ride for great distances in comfort, because the engine is to noisy and the interior is cramped. Another shortcomming is that Volkswagen's are to common. I don't want a car that every mothers son has, and if you look around any large parking lot in this city, you are bound to see at least ten Volkswagen's. Besides being so common, this car is to underpowered for freeway driving. Its almost impossible to pass a car on the expressway at sixty miles per hour, if there is a stiff crosswind blowing, you would think you were on a roller coaster. This is both unpleasant and unsafe.

The third type of car that I wouldn't like to own is one that is cheaply made. Ford Mustangs fall into this class—my family owned one once, and before we got rid of it the muffler fell off at least five times. By the time we sold it six months later, there was rattles in every corner. Meanwhile, the paint had started peeling off, to say nothing of the first layer of chrome on the bumpers. To top it off, whenever the driver made a hard left turn, the door on the passenger's side would fly open. My uncle owns a Cougar, and it doesn't have these problems.

Although I consider myself to be a fairly reasonable person, who can understand that different people like different kinds of cars. I simply cannot understand why anybody would buy the cars I've described here. If their impractical, I don't want them. If their "buggy," forget it. And if their cheap, please leave it on the display floor; because I'm not interested.

Check your answers on p. 116 before continuing.

EXERCISE B. *Proofread the essay you wrote in* step 27, *reading it through once for each type of error listed in this lesson. Then recopy it, using the best introduction and conclusion you wrote, and turn it in to your teacher.*

step 32   Writing a Complete Essay

Applying all the principles you've learned in previous steps, write an essay of approximately 500 words. Follow these steps, checking them off as you finish each one.

...1.   Choose one of the following topics and write a thesis sentence based on it. Be sure that your thesis is at least somewhat arguable or controversial, and that it shows your opinion or position on the question.
   a)   Is TV Violence Really Harmful to Children?
   b)   Why Teenagers Take Drugs
   c)   Should Teenagers Be Allowed to Smoke?
   d)   Is Peace Possible?
   e)   The Importance of Moral Courage
   f)   Should the Draft Be Abolished?

...2.   Jot down the main ideas that support your thesis. Think about your thesis; ask yourself "why?" Decide what ideas prove or explain it. Combine those which are similar. Eliminate any that are not directly related to or don't really support your argument. You should end up with three or four main supporting points. Decide what order they ought to be presented in and number them in sequence.

...3.   Using the chart on page 98, draw up an outline.

    a)   Write the thesis in the space provided and list the main points in the proper blanks, making sure they're in the order you've decided on.

    b)   Starting with the first main point, construct a paragraph outline for each paragraph as follows.

        i)   Write a general statement (the topic sentence) to introduce that main point.

        ii)   Decide what kinds of specifics you will use. Write the type in the blank provided.

        iii)   List the specifics.

        iv)   Check to make sure that all specifics are directly related to the topic sentence. Eliminate any that are not. Add any new ones that occur to you.

        v)   Decide what ordering would be most logical for presenting the specifics. Write the kind you plan to use in the blank provided.

        vi)   Rearrange specifics by numbering them in the order they will appear.

        vii)   Add signal words where necessary.

    c)   Add to the outline any signal words that will be needed to connect the paragraphs.

...4.   Begin to write the essay, following the outline you have constructed.

    a)   Write an introductory paragraph. It must be either *funnel* or *contrast* in construction—depending on which you consider more suitable. Make sure your thesis sentence appears in the introduction. You may *preview* the main points of your essay in the introduction if you wish (see *step 28*).

    b)   Write a paragraph for each of the supporting points. Make sure you explain each specific idea adequately and provide adequate connecting material—using all necessary signal words and connectors. Write a *clincher*, or summary sentence, for any paragraph that needs it.

    c)   Supply any transitions that are needed between paragraphs (see *step 29*).

    d)   Write a conclusion, following the suggestions in *step 30*.

...5.   Go back and double-check your work as follows.

    a)   Place a wavy line under the thesis sentence. Underline the topic sentence and *clincher* in each of the supporting paragraphs.

b) Number the specifics within these paragraphs.

c) Label the introduction either *funnel* or *contrast*. If you have *previewed* your main points in the introduction, number them in order of their appearance in the essay.

d) Circle all signal words and connecting devices.

e) Proofread the entire essay, according to the instructions in *step 31*.

...6. Recopy the essay, ignoring the underlining, numbers, and circles, and submit the final draft to your teacher.

Essay Outline

Thesis Sentence. . . . .
. . . .

First Main Point . . . .

   GS (Topic Sentence) . . . .
   . . . .

   Type(s) of Specifics . . . .

   SP . . . .

   SP . . . .

   SP . . . .

   SP . . . .

   Order of Specifics . . . .

Second Main Point . . . .

   GS (Topic Sentence) . . . .
   . . . .

   Type(s) of Specifics . . . .

   SP . . . .

   SP . . . .

SP . . . .

SP . . . .

Order of Specifics . . . .

Third Main Point . . . .

GS   (Topic Sentence) . . . .

. . . .

Type(s) Of Specifics . . . .

SP . . . .

SP . . . .

SP . . . .

SP . . . .

Order of Specifics . . . .

step 33

Trying It on Your Own

By now you should be able to plan and write a complete essay without being told step-by-step what to do. You should have absorbed the steps and be able to go through the process almost automatically. Prove that you can do it on your own by planning and writing an essay of at least 500 words. Draw up an outline, write the paper, and then proofread it carefully before you recopy and turn it in to your teacher. Choose from the following topics.

a)   How Can One Cope with Loneliness?
b)   Mistakes Parents Make
c)   America's Greatest Problem
d)   Is Censorship Justified?
e)   Should Eighteen-Year-Olds Vote?
f)   What Education Should Be

Answer Key

Answer Key

This answer key has been included to let you check your answers quickly and conveniently. Please do not use it until you have finished working an exercise completely. Otherwise, you will gain nothing from this workbook. Your teacher will not be grading the exercises (except for an occasional complete paragraph or essay). Therefore, looking ahead at the answers will gain you nothing and lose you much. Also, any time your answer differs from the one given here, check carefully to determine why you missed that question. You may sometimes find that you have given a slightly different answer from the one here. Don't panic. Simply try to understand why yours differs. In a few instances, there is more than one possible answer to a question and this will usually be indicated in the key. However, if it is not, and you feel your answer may be equally correct, check with your teacher to make sure.

step 2

1.	G	S	5.	G	S	9.	G	S	13.	G	S
2.	G	S	6.	S	G	10.	S	G	14.	G	S
3.	S	G	7.	G	S	11.	G	S	15.	S	G
4.	G	S	8.	G	S	12.	G	S	16.	G	S

step 3

1.	1	6	5	3	2	4	5.	2	5	3	4	1
2.	5	2	1	3	4		6.	1	4	3	5	2
3.	4	1	2	3	5		7.	2	4	3	1	5
4.	4	5	1	2	3		8.	4	2	5	3	1

step 4   Exercise A

1.	f	3.	b	5.	d	7.	d	9.	b	11.	f	13.	b
2.	d	4.	c	6.	c	8.	e	10.	d	12.	e		

step 4   Exercise B

Answers will vary.
1. transportation
2. pets (or animals)
3. languages (or nationalities)
4. doing chores at home
5. preparing to study (or preparing to write a term paper)
6. earning money at part-time jobs

7. Typing has many advantages for the student.
8. My driver's education teacher is scared to death.

step 5

The ordering of specifics can vary as long as you have the right numbers on each chart. However, the number you place beside the *GS* must correspond to what is given here.

1.			3.		
SP b	SP c		SP a	SP b	
SP e	SP d		SP c	SP d	
SP f	SP h		SP g	SP f	
SP g	SP cars		SP h	SP visiting Washington	
GS cars	GS a		GS visiting Washington	GS e	

2.			4.		
SP a	SP b		SP a	SP c	
SP d	SP e		SP b	SP e	
SP f	SP g		SP d	SP f	
SP h	SP flower		SP g	SP The invention. . .	
GS flower	GS c		GS The invention. . .	GS h	

step 6

Answers will vary. Check to be sure your answers are of the same *type* as those given here. Are all your specifics "contained" in the general item?

1. dolls, games, electric trains, blocks
2. baseball, basketball, football, soccer
3. gathering equipment, soaping the car, scrubbing the wheels, rinsing the car off thoroughly
4. joining the Pep club, voting in school elections, working on the drama productions, serving as publicity chairman of the Honor Society
5. scanning the headlines, checking scores on the sports page, chuckling over the comics, disagreeing with the editorial page thoughtfully
6. We travel more than our parents did. Young people can get away from home easily. We choke on smog created by auto exhaust. A shopping trip downtown is easy and convenient.
7. He treats his students fairly. He shows interest in each member of the class. He is intelligent, well-informed, and articulate. He sees his students as people, not things.

step 7

1. The student of today has many worries.
2. Our trip to Washington, D. C. was the high point of the summer.
3. An American adolescent derives his moral standards from many sources.
4. A well-planned mass transit network offers many advantages to a city and its citizens.

5. An alligator must have a natural-like environment in order to survive in captivity.
6. In many of its limitations, our school's dress code is unfair to students.
7. In short, though I don't know what death is like, since I have never experienced it, I am almost certain that some situations in a teenager's daily life are worse than dying.

step 8

Answers will vary. Check to make sure your answers are of the same type as those given here. Is your topic sentence general enough to summarize all the specifics? Is it a complete sentence?

1. Hunting appeals to many types of people.
2. Reading a textbook assignment effectively requires careful work.
3. Photography is an interesting and profitable hobby.
4. Hunting is a necessary part of good wildlife conservation.

step 9

1. b f   2. d f   3. c f   4. b e   5. d e   6. b f   7. c e g

step 10

Answers will vary. Check to be sure your answers are similar in form to those suggested here. Are your specifics all "contained" in the general statement given?

1. He meets many famous people and goes to many glamorous places.
   He must often work long hours on the set.
   He is constantly hounded by fans and is rarely alone.
   Though the challenge of a good role is great, it requires much work.
2. I would respect him.
   I would allow him to make his own decisions whenever possible.
   I would be interested in the things that concern him.
   I would be firm, but not unreasonable.
3. There is no better way for the student to learn to drive well.
   Parents often do not have time to teach their teenagers to drive.
   Such training has been shown to reduce the teenage accident rate.
   If a student has had driver's training, his auto insurance rates are lower.

step 11

Did you use the general statement given as the first sentence of your paragraph? Did you indent the first line? Did you explain each specific in an additional sentence or two?

step 12

Is your general statement a complete sentence? Are all your specifics "contained" in the general statement?

step 13

Did you indent the first line and keep the margins straight? Did you clarify each specific with extra explanatory and connecting information? Did you underline the topic sentence and number the specifics, as shown in the example?

Step 14   Exercise B

Answers will vary. Check your paragraph against the example below, which contains adequate connecting information.

While television shows are reasonably good, the commercials that accompany them are a disgrace. One of the many bad features of commercials is their loudness. They seem to be twice as loud as the program and the viewer is almost deafened when they come on. Any attempt at conversation during commercials is futile. Commercials also take up too much time and are repeated too often. The impression one usually gets is that the shows are sandwiched in between long periods of advertising, all of it the same. Often commercials interrupt a show at a particularly inappropriate time. Just when the program is getting exciting, just as the plot begins to thicken, or the long-awaited star is about to come on, the announcer reports that "we will be back after this message." Too many commercials insult the viewers intelligence by presenting unrealistic situations and senseless dialogue. Tornadoes and doves rip in and out of kitchens, white knights gallop through backyards, and employees declare to their bosses that they have bad breath. It seems that, rather than inducing the viewer to buy a product, commercials are deliberately planned to turn him against it.

step 15

Is your general statement a complete sentence? Are all your specifics related to the general statement? Did you underline the topic sentence and number the specifics?

step 16   Exercise A

1.   *Topic Sentence:*   The owner of a pet alligator should protect it by placing it in a pen of some sort.

> *Clincher:* All of these dangers can be eliminated if the owner keeps his pet in a fenced off pond or in a pen.

2. *Topic Sentence:* The important question of whom to have as a friend must be answered by the teen himself—not by his parents.
   Clincher: If parents have faith in the teenager's judgement they will generally find that it pays off in the long-run, because the child will often choose friends sensibly and, even when he makes a mistake, he can learn much from it.

3. *Topic Sentence:* An understanding of history helps us to realize that our problems are nothing new.
   Clincher: Clearly, today's problems aren't really so new; they simply appear in different forms.

4. *Topic Sentence:* Good notetaking is indispensable to efficient study.
   No Clincher.

5. *Topic Sentence:* My greatest disappointment, I think, was the time I went to camp in Vermont.
   Clincher: Perhaps my experience would have been less disappointing had I known before I arrived what the camp was really like.

6. *Topic Sentence* (and *Clincher*): The Gateway Arch is a truly spectacular tourist spot. (*The first sentence in this paragraph presents specifics, and is not a topic sentence.*)

7. *Topic Sentence:* Often the starting time of a sports event is delayed or changed because of television.
   No clincher.

8. *Topic Sentence* (and *Clincher*): Every high school student, therefore, should learn to type because of the many advantages which typing has over script. (*As in* 6, *the first sentence presents specifics.*)

step 16   Exercise B

Did you place the general statement (topic sentence) at the end of your paragraph? Is it a complete sentence? Is it general enough to include all the specifics? Are all your specifics directly related to this statement? Did you remember to underline the topic sentence and number the specifics?

step 16   Exercise C

Did you place the general statement (topic sentence) at the beginning of the paragraph? Is it a complete sentence? Does it include all the specifics contained in the paragraph? Are all your specifics directly related to the general statement? Did you write a clincher sentence at the end? Does it restate the topic sentence in *different words*? Did you underline both topic sentence and clincher and number the specifics?

step 17　Exercise A

Note that some of the specifics fall into more than one category.

1.			2.			3.		
	a.	fact		a.	fact		a.	fact or reason
	b.	incident		b.	example or		b.	incident
	c.	fact or reason			incident		c.	example or
	d.	fact, reason,		c.	fact			reason
		or example		d.	example		d.	example or
	e.	reason		e.	incident			reason
	f.	reason						

step 17　Exercise B

1.	examples or facts	6.	reasons or examples
2.	reasons	7.	incident
3.	facts	8.	reasons or examples
4.	facts	9.	incident
5.	incident	10.	facts

step 17　Exercise C

Is your general statement a complete sentence. Did you use *facts* as the specifics in your paragraph? Are all your facts related directly to the general statement? Did you write "facts" in the appropriate blank on your outline? Did you provide adequate connecting explanation between your specifics? Did you underline the topic sentence and number the specifics?

step 17　Exercise D

Is your general statement a complete sentence? Did you use *examples* as the specifics in your paragraph? Are all your examples directly related to the general statement? Did you write "examples" in the appropriate blank on your outline? Did you provide adequate connecting explanation between your examples? Did you underline the topic sentence and number the specifics?

step 17　Exercise E

Is your topic sentence a general statement of the main idea of the paragraph and not part of the incident you use to explain it? Is your supporting incident explained in detail? Have you used only *one* incident? Did you underline the topic sentence and clincher?

step 17　Exercise F

Is your general statement a complete sentence? Have you underlined it? Do all of your specifics answer the question "why"? Did you write "reasons" in the appropriate blank on your outline? Did you provide adequate connecting detail between your reasons?

step 18

1. examples, incident, reasons
2. examples, incident, reasons
3. examples, reasons, facts
4. examples, incident, reasons
5. steps in a process
6. examples, incident, facts
7. examples, incident, reasons
8. analysis, examples, incident, facts
9. incident, descriptive details
10. definition, examples, reasons, comparison/contrast
11. examples, reasons, quotation
12. examples, incident, reasons, comparison/contrast

step 19   Exercise A

1. comparison/contrast, type b
2. time
3. comparison/contrast, type a
4. importance
5. comparison/contrast, type b
6. time
7. importance

step 19   Exercise B

1. time (2 4 1 3)
2. comparison/contrast: either
   type a (1 3 4 2 5 6) or
   type b (1 6 3 5 4 2)
3. position (2 4 6 1 3 5)
4. time or difficulty (2 4 3 1)
5. time (2 1 5 4 3)
6. problem to answer (5 2 1 4 3)

step 19   Exericse C

Have you used a different order of specifics in each of your three paragraphs? Did you write in the appropriate blanks the *kind* and *order* to be used? Are all of your general statements complete sentences? Did you underline topic sentences and clinchers and number specifics? Did you explain each specific adequately and provide connecting information? *Save these paragraphs. You'll need them in* step 20.

step 20   Exercise A

1. a) In addition (listing)   b) Furthermore (listing)   c) Besides (listing)
   d) Finally (listing)   e) Therefore (results)
2. a) First (listing)   b) Second (listing)   c) on the other hand (contrast)

d) Next (listing)   e) however (contrast)

3.   a) For instance (examples)   b) Thus (results)   c) On the other hand (contrast)   d) For example (examples)

step 20   Exercise C

Did you write the type of specifics you planned to use in the appropriate blank on your outline. Did you indicate what order you were going to use? Did you supply the needed signal words?

step 21   Exercise A

1.   b (for instance)
2.   b (he. . .it)
3.   a (But. . .those)
4.   b (Consequently)
5.   a (However. . .others)
6.   a (Ever since that time)
7.   b (another)

step 21   Exercise B

Answers may vary.
1.   *He* practiced law in my home town for thirty-five years.
2.   *Then* (or *Next*), find the dog and lure him into the tub.
3.   *For example,* he turns the novel into a play at several points.
4.   *This action* had an effect on most of the countries in the Western World.
5.   *One disadvantage* is that (or *For example,*) you are tied down to one boy or girl and have no opportunity to get to know anyone else.
6.   One of the things that made *him* a great president was that (or *For example,*) he inspired the youth of this country.
7.   *This brave man* (or *For example, he*) had to place himself in a machine that could become a coffin travelling at 600 miles per hour at any moment.
8.   *But* (or *However* or *On the other hand*), at Madison High *they* are not allowed to smoke at all.
9.   *In addition* (or *Also*), she sings very well.
10.   *Therefore* (or *As a result*), he is not qualified for the position he holds.
11.   *Then* you are ready to begin writing.

step 21   Exercise C

Check your paragraph to make sure that the relationships among the ideas are made perfectly clear and that it flows smoothly from one idea to the next.

step 22

Here is the paragraph with errors corrected. Each corrected error has been underlined.

The way one studies for a test is very important. (*Did you notice that the original version contains no topic sentence?*) The student should first of all find a quiet, well-lighted place with no distracting noises. The place he chooses should be level and large enough for all the books, papers, and materials that he needs. All these materials should be gathered before beginning to work, since it is a waste of time to constantly have to stop and go running after a book or ruler. The time one chooses to study is also important. Generally it should be at a time convenient to the student, but it should not begin too late in the evening. Breaks in study time are very necessary, since one cannot be expected to concentrate for long periods without a rest. In fact, research studies show that one's study is more efficient if he works for about forty-five minutes and takes a ten-minute snack break. One should be careful, though, that his "break" time does not exceed the amount of time he spends actually studying. Once the student has found the proper environment for his study and has established a time to begin, the real work starts. Studying is a complex process that requires concentration. If one has textbook assignments to read, this reading should be done actively, with an attempt to remember the main points of the assignment. (*The next sentence in the original is an unrelated specific; eliminate it.*) If one has lecture notes to review, he should do more than skim over them half-heartedly. The good student will be thinking of possible test questions based on these notes. By doing this, he is usually not totally surprised when he reads the examination questions. If one takes care to follow these steps when he studies, he will find that the effort pays off in better grades and more free time.

step 24   Exercise A

Introduction

> A person applying for the Peace Corps will find he has to go through a complex procedure. This includes meeting certain qualifications, responding to questionnaires and examinations, and going through a period of training.

There are several qualifications which an applicant must have. First, [1]he must be at least eighteen years old and a citizen of the United States. [2]He can be married, but if both he and his wife want to serve, they must have no children under the age of eighteen. A third

ANSWER KEY   111

qualification is [3]vocational skill. (This) means that the applicant must already know how to do something like teach or farm, because the program has no provision for training him. (However,) [4]neither a college education nor knowledge of a foreign language is required. (Another) qualification is that [5]he must not have any serious physical mental or emotional disturbances. (Most important of all though,) [6]he must be willing to work for two years.

(If) his qualifications meet Peace Corps standards, the applicant must provide various kinds of written information. (First,) [1]he must fill out a questionnaire, listing his skills, hobbies, how much education he has had and where, his special interests, and his work background, if any. The applicant [2]must (also) provide references from friends, teachers, and/or employers. (Furthermore,) [3]he must take placement tests— which are noncompetitive and test his aptitudes and ability to learn foreign languages. A volunteer is picked for training on the basis of the information he gives on the questionnaire, the aptitude and ability he shows on the tests, and his references.

(After) taking the tests, a chosen volunteer must go through a training period of eight to ten weeks at a United States college. (During this time,) [1]the volunteer is taught a great deal about the country in which he will be working. He studies its language, history, and culture. [2]He is (also) given technical, physical, and health training to enable him to remain healthy while living like the natives of the country where he will be working. (Another) important part of the training is [3]learning about the history of the United States and the meaning of democracy. (This) enables the volunteer to explain our system of government to others when he is asked. When the period of training ends, final selections of volunteers are made.

Conclusion { After the final selections, the successful volunteer is sent to a foreign country, where he serves for two years. By the time (these) two years are completed, he understands that the initial selection and training process was worthwhile.

step 24   Exercise B

Introduction { Today's teenager encounters many problems in his diversified life. (Nevertheless,) few teenagers ever discuss their problems with their parents—the two people who love them most and want the best for them—but prefer to talk about them with friends. Most adults feel they are aware of their teenager's problems and readily available to help solve them. (But) the teenager often fails to bring his problems before his parents because he senses in them distrust, preoccupation, and a lack of understanding—all of which seem to be contributing factors in this unfortunate failure to communicate.

Many adolescents feel that an older person, such as a parent, is unable to relate to the problems of the present-day youth. (Some) parents fail to understand because of the [1]different environment in which they grew up, which produced different experiences and problems. (For example,) most parents see "going steady" as undesirable, even though most teenagers do it. The reason they dislike this practice is that when they were young it meant the couple was planning to be engaged soon. Now, of course, (this) is not the case. (Other) parents tend to [2]underestimate the pressures on today's students, such as the necessity of getting superior grades in high school. When they were ready to go to college, the main requirement was having enough money. (Today,) however, it is necessary for a student to be in the upper fifth of his class if he is to enter a competitive university. (Such things) may be extremely important to the teen, yet can seem merely foolish to an adult who does not realize the seriousness of the problem. [3]Parents (also) fail to realize the change in life style their teenagers are making. They often cannot accept the fact that the dependent adolescent is changing into a self-reliant adult. (Along with this) change emerge added responsibilities and privileges. (However,) when giving advice, many a parent acts as though he were addressing a young child rather than someone who is almost an adult. Due to this lack of understanding on the parents' part, the teenager feels he has no choice but to turn to his friends, who have similar problems and are more apt to understand him. Simple misunderstandings (then,) such as those mentioned here, may become major stumbling blocks to attempts at communication between teenager and parent.

Distrust is another cause for (this) lack of communication. While parents may say they trust their teenagers, their actions often indicate otherwise. (For example,) [1]many parents listen in on their children's phone calls or open their mail, because they do not trust them to behave themselves properly. (Also,) [2]parents frequently impose unreasonable restrictions on their adolescent's activities, simply because they do not trust his judgement. No young person is going to talk openly to an adult who shows no faith in his intelligence or his actions. (Furthermore,) [3]many parents demonstrate quite clearly that they are not deserving of trust themselves. It may be that they simply repeat to another person in the family something told to them in confidence, but to many teens this is an act of disloyalty. When (this) kind of mutual distrust develops, the lines of communication break down.

(Another) reason the teenager does not bring his problems to his parents is that they are often too busy or too wrapped up in their own lives to give him the attention he needs. To some parents, [1]social commitments are more important than being at home to discuss the problems of their children. (Or) ²(they) feel that they can fulfill their responsibilities by giving their children money and a car. Some fathers, (for example,) are so busy working to provide these material comforts for their families that they have no time left to spend with their children. ³Even the television set can become an obstacle between parents and children. It is next to impossible for the teenager to bring his problems before his parents when they are sitting glued to the screen all evening, every evening. Parents who are too involved with their own activities to notice their teenager's problem force him to seek advice elsewhere. (In such families,) lack of communication is due to the parents' selfishness.

Conclusion

Lack of communication between the generations will continue until adults realize that teenagers are maturing individuals who need attention, understanding, and respectful trust. Lack of any of (these) elements in the parents' attitude will always create barriers between teenager and parent. And (these) barriers must be broken and conquered before meaningful communication can begin.

step 24   Exercise C

Thesis Sentence: But the teenager often fails to bring his problems before his parents because he senses in them distrust, preoccupation, and a lack of understanding—all of which seem to be contributing factors in this unfortunate failure to communicate.

First Main Point: parents' lack of understanding
  GS *(Topic Sentence)* Many adolescents feel that an older person, such as a parent, is unable to relate to the problems of the present-day youth.
  SP different environment in which parents grew up
  SP underestimation of the pressures on today's students
  SP failure to realize the change of life style their children are making

Second Main Point: mutual distrust
  GS *(Topic Sentence)* Distrust is another cause for this lack of communication.
  SP actions that demonstrate parents' lack of trust in their children
  SP imposition of unreasonable restrictions on teens
  SP untrustworthy actions of parents themselves

Third Main Point: parents' preoccupation with their own activities
  GS *(Topic Sentence)* Another reason the teenager does not bring his problems to his parents is that they are often too busy or too wrapped up in their own lives to give him the attention he needs.
  SP greater interest in their own social commitments than in their children's problems

SP attempts to fulfill their family obligations with material gifts
SP the interference of television

step 25

1.	b	6.	a	
2.	b	7.	a	
3.	b	8.	a	
4.	a	9.	b	
5.	b	10.	a	

step 26

Does your thesis sentence meet the requirements listed in *step 25*? Did you indicate the type and order of specifics you plan to use by writing them in the appropriate blanks? Did you add the necessary signal words to your outline?

step 27

Does your thesis appear in the introductory paragraph? Did you use a complete paragraph for each of your supporting points? Did you write a good concluding paragraph? Did you place a wavy line under the thesis, underline topic sentences, number specifics, and circle signal words?

step 28   Exercise A

Does your *funnel* introduction begin with an idea that is more general than any other in the paragraph? Is the last idea in your paragraph the thesis? Is it the most specific idea in the introduction? Have you provided the steps in between—gradually becoming more and more specific as you move toward the thesis? Do your ideas flow smoothly from one to another? (This is a frequent weakness of funnel paragraphs; you may want to review the types of connectors, *steps 20* and *21*.)

step 28   Exercise B

Does your *contrast* introduction fall into two parts—the first presenting a commonly held belief, and the second presenting a thesis which contradicts or modifies this belief? Did you use some sort of signal word to indicate the contradiction? Did you explain in detail (several sentences) the commonly held belief that begins your paragraph?

step 28   Exercise C

1. *Thesis:*   last sentence
   Type: contrast
   Factors: lack of understanding, automatic distrust, constant preoccu-
               pation

2. *Thesis:* last sentence
   Type: contrast
   Factors: religion, morality, choice of friends

3. *Thesis:* last sentence
   Type: funnel
   Factors: physical prowess, more responsible, mature

4. *Thesis:* last sentence
   Type: contrast
   Factors: young mans wants to become an auto mechanic, young woman wants to get married, young man wants a career in the military service

step 29   Exercise A

1. b (also, this)
2. a (Another)
3. a (On the other hand)
4. a (this, however)
5. a (As a result, this)
6. a (these)
7. a (But, they, such)
8. b (Nevertheless)
9. a (Likewise)
10. b (First)

step 30

Were you careful to avoid repeating your ideas in exactly the same words as they were expressed earlier in the essay?

step 31   Exercise A

Here is the essay, with the errors corrected:

There are over a quarter of a million automobiles sold in the United States each year. Many types are available; foreign cars and American cars, convertibles and sedans, big cars and little cars. This variety is the result of the wide range of taste of the driving population. There are three kinds of cars which don't suit my taste at all, and which I would never own. One type is impractical, another is little and ugly, and a third is poorly made.

An example of an impractical car is the Excalibur SS. Perhaps you have never seen one of these cars. It bears a strong resemblance to the Dusenberg of years ago or to an old MG, early 1951 or 1952. One of the things I don't like about it is that it only comes in a convertible model. That's fine in the summer or on a sunny day, but when it rains or when winter comes it's rather impractical. Winter is perhaps the roughest though, mainly because the car is not even equipped with a heater. And the softtop has plastic side windows and a plastic rear window that leak and yellow in the sun and become brittle with age. This car is fitted with a 327 cubic inch engine from the Corvette Stingray. But it doesn't weigh more than 2000 pounds, compared to the Corvette, which weighs approximately 3200 pounds this year. With over 350 horsepower and so little weight, the Excalibur is very dangerous. You can't come near controlling it on acceleration around curves or on a panic stop. Combining these shortcomings with a $10,000 price tag, you have a very impractical car.

Another car that I wouldn't want is one of those ugly little foreign "bugs" you see everywhere. The Volkswagen is a good example. This simply isn't my idea of a car with good looks. In addition, it's too small for safety. If you were hit in the side by a large car or by a truck, you'd be finished. You also can't ride for great distances in comfort, because the engine is too noisy and the interior is cramped. Another shortcoming is that Volkswagens are too common. I don't want a car that every mother's son has, and if you look around any large parking lot in this city, you are bound to see at least ten Volkswagens. Besides being so common, this car is too underpowered for freeway driving. It's almost impossible to pass a car on the expressway at sixty miles per hour, and if there is a stiff crosswind blowing, you would think you were on a roller coaster. This is both unpleasant and unsafe.

The third type of car that I wouldn't like to own is one that is cheaply made. Ford Mustangs fall into this class. My family owned one once, and before we got rid of it the muffler fell off at least five times. By the time we sold it six months later, there were rattles in every corner. Meanwhile, the paint had started peeling off, to say nothing of the first layer of chrome on the bumpers. To top it off, whenever the driver made a hard left turn, the door on the passenger's side would fly open. (*The last sentence in the original version is an unrelated specific; eliminate it.*)

Although I consider myself to be a fairly reasonable person, who can understand that different people like different kinds of cars, I simply cannot understand why anybody would by the cars I've described here. If they're impractical, I don't want them. If they're "buggy," forget it. And if they're cheap, please leave them on the display floor, because I'm not interested.

If you did not spot all of these errors when proofreading, you may have a weakness in grammar, punctuation, or spelling. See your teacher for additional help.